Edwin Lutyens

ARCHITECTURAL
Monographs 6

Edwin Lutyens

Academy Editions · London/St. Martin's Press · New York

Subscriptions and Editorial Offices
7/8 Holland Street, London W8

Publisher
Dr Andreas Papadakis

Editor
David Dunster

Acknowledgements

The editor would like to thank *Country Life* for permission to reproduce from its collection many photographs that were taken just after the completion of the buildings. The views of interiors are now the only real documentary evidence of this aspect of Lutyens' work. The date which follows the individual credit, *CL*, refers to the original date of publication in *Country Life*.

The Honourable Mrs Clayre Ridley kindly gave her permission for extracts from the letters of Sir Edwin to Lady Lutyens and Mrs J. G. Links kindly gave her permission for the extract from Lady Lutyens' letter to Sir Edwin.

Mrs Margaret Richardson of the Drawings Collection of the British Architectural Library at the Royal Institute of British Architects gave every assistance and the Library permitted the use of photographs of Lutyens' archive material.

Photographs which are not individually credited were taken either by Peter Inskip or David Dunster, with the exception of the cover and the colour gatefolds which were by Andre Goulancourt.

All of the plans were redrawn by Eleni Laskou under the supervision of Peter Inskip, with the exception of El Guadalperal, redrawn by Nigel Montague, and Lindisfarne, Marshcourt and Goddards, redrawn by Sarah Halliday.

Finally, we would like to thank all present owners of Lutyens' homes for their assistance with the preparation of this Monograph. We would stress that their homes are private and point out that Castle Drogo, Great Dixter, Great Maytham, and Lindisfarne are at present open to the public.

Published in Great Britain in 1986 by
Academy Editions, 7/8 Holland Street, London W8

© 1979, 1986 Architectural Monographs
and Academy Editions

ISBN 0 85670 422 9 (paper)
ISBN 0 85670 891 7 (cased)

Published in the United States of America in 1986 by St Martin's Press, 175 Fifth Avenue, New York, NY 10010

Library of Congress Catalog Card Number 86-024540
ISBN 0 312 23919 X (paper)
ISBN 0 312 23918 1 (cased)

Printed and bound in Hong Kong

Contents

Front cover: The Salutation, 1911 east front.
Back cover: Le Bois des Moutiers, 1898, view of entrance over garden wall.
Inside front cover: Deanery Garden, 1901 view of the fountain courtyard from the garden.
Inside back cover: The Pleasaunce 1899, stable gate. (All photographs Andre Goulancourt).
Frontispiece: Sir Edwin Lutyens 1869-1944, from the mezzotint by Lawrence Josset of the oil painting by Meredith Frampton.

Foreword

This issue of Architectural Monographs is something of a departure. Sir Edwin Lutyens (1869-1944) has never been cannonised by architectural historians as a predecessor of the Modern Movement. Indeed, he stood completely aloof from it to the extent that Henry-Russell Hitchcock has dubbed him 'the last traditionalist'. He displayed no interest in either the free plan or advanced technological symbolism. His vast output of over 300 buildings and projects shows a continuing fascination with traditional constructional techniques and borrowing from the past, not simply as an elevational overlay on a 'modern' plan but in the scale and detailing of the functionally distinct rooms.

The reader cannot expect, then, a direct connection with that tradition of modernism still the staple diet of teaching programmes in schools of architecture. And as if to make matters worse Lutyens designed to requirements which today are almost non-existent — the large country house is the sample of his work catalogued here. With so much against him, the absence of interest in Lutyens since his death can be no surprise. Perhaps now that the course of architecture has rejected the frigid application of Modern Movement thought to all problems, those experiments which Lutyens undertook can be viewed dispassionately, for their merits and not as the point when real architecture stopped, as some neo-Imperialist historians would have it.

In Peter Inskip's essay the qualities of Lutyens' houses and their chronological development are laid out from the modernist point of view. To take one obvious example, Lutyens has much to offer in terms of the plan's hierarchy. The sucession of spatial events within are often carefully graded by volume and lighting and present what might tentatively be called a technology of planning; that is an exposition of architectural devices whereby the room and the corridor are thematically, some would say theatrically, linked. Add to this example, and at somewhat the same level, the remarkable way in which access and axis approach house and garden, taking into account the contingencies of site and orientation. Grey Walls has been the example perhaps most frequently touted to justify interest in Lutyens, but there are many others. All the plans in this issue have been redrawn with particular attention to this aspect of his works. These lay bare the fracture between the back and front which allowed Lutyens the intellectual space to play with the plan and perhaps was the occasion for his virtuoso designs which extend the vocabulary of architecture. His houses rarely have a central space commanding a hierarchy of rooms. The fracture of back and front by which the forces of the outside can be allowed almost complete dominion over the plan behind must mean that a centre is not possible. Often the buildings seem schizoid, a vernacularised domestic garden side and a symmetrical and formal entrance court. Tigbourne springs readily to mind as an example.

The hints of this fracture seem underlined by the detailing: often quirky, sometimes brilliant, always skillful. A massive re-evaluation of Lutyens is obviously underway. Following the pioneering discursions of his work by Venturi and Greenberg, we can now expect a great increase in his critical bibliography. Whether the work is for a class of such disgusting affluence that it is tainted by the immorality of commerce or whether the work is of such skill and brilliance that it opens up possibilities in the design discourse to reunite function and decoration are questions we hope this issue will fuel.

Historically a figure like Lutyens may open up for practising architects an understanding of past works, revealing that specifically English quality of pragmatic idealism found in his work as much as in the work of Sir John Soane, Sir John Vanbrugh and Nicholas Hawksmoor. The issues of eclecticism and morality may yet find resolution here.

Opposite
Mr Drewe's bathroom,
Castle Drogo, Devon
(CL 1945)

Lutyens' Houses
Peter Inskip

Opposite
1 Deanery Garden 1901 –
  the house as castle (CL
  c.1905)

In this essay I shall try to deal with certain categories by which Lutyens' work can be approached. Each of the houses is a complex and sometimes eclectic enterprise, trying both to solve the needs of the client and to expand a series of architectural ideas which preoccupied Lutyens throughout his life. While I would not want to put forward a case for the archetypal Lutyens' house, it is possible to identify a group of common characteristics. They represent techniques evolved to solve problems directly related to the country house programme and his clients' particular requirements. In addition there is in all the houses evidence of an intention to increase the apparent size of the building and a desire to develop the relationship between the house and its garden, sometimes by extending the geometric structure of the house out into the garden, sometimes by treating the houses as metaphoric castles protected by garden elements in the form of fictive fortifications. The plans in this monograph have been extensively redrawn to illustrate this point.[1] A note is added on the use Lutyens made of paradox to control the building through planning as well as its use through interior decoration and what I have termed 'archaeology'.

Sir Edwin Landseer Lutyens was born in 1869, the son of a retired soldier turned sporting artist, and named after his father's hero, Sir Edwin Landseer. Lutyens was the exact contemporary of Frank Lloyd Wright, one year younger than C. R. Mackintosh and twelve years younger than C. F. A. Voysey. After virtually no formal education followed by a period studying vernacular buildings around his home at Thursley in Surrey with Gertrude Jekyll (who had invented or rather revived the image of the informal English Cottage Garden) he entered the office of Sir Ernest George in 1887 where among others he met his later collaborator on New Delhi, Herbert Baker. Only two years later he set up in practice on his own account and between 1889 and 1912 built many outstanding houses. He continued to accept domestic commissions after his appointment in 1912 to design the Viceroy's House at New Delhi, even though the emphasis of his growing practice shifted to large commercial buildings such as the Midland Bank in the City (1928). In these houses he continued to use many of the ideas worked out in his early buildings. After the Great War he became a principal architect to the Imperial War Graves Commission, designing both the Cenotaph in Whitehall and the Memorial to the Missing at Thiepval in France. During the Second World War, while president of the Royal Academy, he drew up plans

Quotation of his own and
contemporary works:
2 Heathcote 1906 (CL
  1910)
3 Little Thakeham 1902
  (CL 1909)
4 Homewood 1901
5 Standen by Philip
  Webb 1891

4

5

for the reconstruction of London after the Blitz. He died in January 1944, surrounded by his drawings of Liverpool Roman Catholic Cathedral – a building intended to rival St Peter's in scale – the construction of which started in 1933 only to be abandoned on grounds of cost in 1959 with just the crypt complete.

Lutyens' houses do not innovate conceptually but are a brilliant synthesis of ideas he shared with his contemporaries. They all possess the same basic plan elaborated to accommodate the specific programme and overlaid with stylistic quotations from historical and contemporary sources, as well as his own previous works, producing an 'original' design. This basic plan is common to the majority of his projects for houses in Great Britain, Europe and America and the pattern established in those built early in his career around Godalming in Surrey is modified only in response to the differing requirements of more affluent clients and the development of the group of architectual ideas he was exploring. The administrative and symbolic function of the Indian palaces he designed places them beyond the boundaries of this volume. They form a separate group because of their administrative nature and completely different domestic organisation.

Stylistic quotations sometimes come through directly to the final form but often act as catalysts in preliminary schemes, a stage in the evolution of design. For example the wrot iron balconies inserted between the bastions on the terrace at Heathcote (1906) can be seen to borrow from his earlier staircase at Little Thakeham (1902); this in turn is derived from Richard Norman Shaw's house at 170 Queensgate (1888) and is an historical quotation from Vanbrugh's houses, such as Grimsthorpe Castle of 1722. Likewise the form of the three weatherboarded gables at Homewood (1901) owes much to Philip Webb's work at Joldwyns and Standen (1891). The use of the quotation as a catalyst

2

3

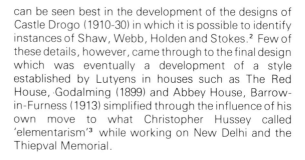

6

7

8

can be seen best in the development of the designs of Castle Drogo (1910-30) in which it is possible to identify instances of Shaw, Webb, Holden and Stokes.[2] Few of these details, however, came through to the final design which was eventually a development of a style established by Lutyens in houses such as The Red House, Godalming (1899) and Abbey House, Barrow-in-Furness (1913) simplified through the influence of his own move to what Christopher Hussey called 'elementarism'[3] while working on New Delhi and the Thiepval Memorial.

More important than the stylistic details and compositional ideas derived from antecedents is that his attitude to design can be seen as a direct continuation and combination of two lines of thought in the nineteenth century. Firstly, the Gothic Revival High Church architects' provision of a moral basis for truth in architecture, that is the importance of the building responding to its functional requirements, the nature of its materials and the site; secondly, the English water-colour school typified by such architects as George Devey (1820-86) who had studied the vernacular to see how picturesque architecture was really composed in both detailing and massing. It was this current idea of first-hand study that prompted Lutyens to visit seventeenth and eighteenth-century vernacular farmhouses with Gertrude Jekyll, at that time gathering material for such books as *Old West Surrey*,[4] and led him to discover the monumental qualities found in primitive simplicity, a relationship which he later clearly reiterated, for example, in the hall of Little Thakeham (1902).

Many of Lutyens' preoccupations can be traced, through the work of Philip Webb which he much admired, to the rationalism of William Butterfield's country vicarages, themselves carefully derived from the requirements of their occupants and the capabilities of the materials used in their construction. This partially accounts for the importance Lutyens attached to a functional plan. However, the influence of the picturesque meant that when he adapted Webb's Joldwyns and Standen elevations for his own design for Homewood at Knebworth, he abandoned the rational eighteenth-century sliding sash window, which had been taken up by the Gothic Revival architects because of the ventilation control it gave, and reverted to the seventeenth-century leaded light casement set between mullions and transoms.

In other instances, such as in the oak stair at Deanery Garden, he adopted the constructional integrity of Webb and Butterfield but his self-conscious expression

of every joint and dowel reveals a concern more with visual than constructional integrity. Often this led to an unnecessary over-exaggeration of the scale of exposed timbers, examples being the hall at Deanery Garden or the gallery at Munstead Wood, and to the concealment of steelwork in the apparently massive granite construction of Castle Drogo. His habit of burying service and rainwater pipes in masonry walls is certainly a divergence from the rational tradition as is now being appreciated with regret by the owners of Nashdom and Ednaston.

Quotation as a catalyst - Castle Drogo 1910-30

6 Sketch 1910: a Norman tower, the Lindisfarne battery and Holden's Bristol Library 1905 (Peter Inskip collection)

7 The Red House, Godalming 1899

8 Staircase window as built, visual integrity

9

However, the greatest influence on Lutyens, both stylistically and professionally, was Richard Norman Shaw (1831-1912). Between 1871 and 1890 Shaw developed the style of his houses from a Tudor vernacular (Leyswood 1871), through an early eighteenth-century manner (170 Queensgate, Kensington 1888) to baroque classicism (Chesters 1890). Lutyens paralleled this completely between 1896 and 1906 with Orchards (1897), Great Maytham (1907) and Heathcote (1905). The turning back to Shaw's earlier work for inspiration rather than to his new-found classicism was because of Lutyens' preoccupation in 1896 with the vernacular. It is only through details such as chimney-pieces or stair balustrades that classicism gradually appeared in his work before the turn of the century. While trying to resolve the approach to Grey Walls with various orthoganal arrangements in 1901 he visited Chesters and was so influenced by Shaw's curved screen across the side of the house that he adapted it to a vernacular eighteenth-century form so that a diagonal drive could terminate at the side of his H-shape plan. The details, however, are related to Lutyens' 'Wrennaissance' style, later developed at Great Maytham, and it was not until 1906 that Heathcote represented an experiment in full Shavian baroque classicism.

Nevertheless both architects willingly reverted to idioms that they had used earlier, dependent on task or client. However excited Lutyens was at the discovery of 'the high game of Palladio' at Heathcote, he continued to design houses in vernacular, Georgian and classical styles throughout his life. Even if his preference was for houses on the lines of Ednaston (1912),[5] he still accepted commissions restricted to a specific style; Castle Drogo is contemporary with his imperial classicism at New Delhi, and Halnaker is a rendered, vernacular house built as late as 1936, while he was designing his last great classical house, Middleton Park (1938). For Lutyens, Shaw provided the model of the great architect. Extrovert, with considerable influence through a large number of pupils, a big office and a prolific output, he was the antithesis of Webb or the English Free School architects with their small offices executing domestic commissions. This admiration even led Lutyens to take on the lease of Shaw's old office at 29, Bloomsbury Square.

The client

Shaw worked for highly successful, self-made industrialists, merchants and the intelligentsia rather than the old aristocracy. At Cragside Lord Armstrong, the industrialist and inventor, was a typical client. Although Lutyens' earliest commissions were from family friends and the Jekyll circle around Godalming, after 1900 his clients were similar to Shaw's: Herbert Johnson (Marshcourt) was a stockbroker, Henry and Mark Farrer (The Salutation and 4, St James's Square, London) the Hon Cecil Baring (Lambay Castle) and Alfred Mildmay (Mothecombe House) were bankers.

9 Staircase, Deanery Garden 1901 (CL c.1905)

10

13

11

14

Shaw and Lutyens
10 Leyswood by Shaw 1870 (BN, March 31 1871)
11 170, Queensgate, Kensington by Shaw 1888
12 Chesters by Shaw 1890
13 Orchards 1897 - English Free School
14 Great Maytham 1907 -Wrennaissance (CL c.1929)
15 Heathcote 1906 -Baroque Classicism (CL 1910)

12

15

Politics were represented by the Hon Alfred Littleton (Grey Walls and Wittersham House) and trade by Julius Drewe (Castle Drogo). Often a commission for a house came with one for a client's offices; in 1913 W. G. Player approached Lutyens for the design of both Ednaston Manor and new offices at the Nottingham tobacco factory, and in 1924 Reginald McKenna brought the commission for the Midland Bank and Mells Park House. When aristocrats appear in the list they are either recent ascendants (Lord Beatty at Hanover Lodge) or backed by American heiresses (Prince Alexis Dolgorouki at Nashdom) or family (his mother-in-law, the Dowager Countess of Lytton at Homewood) or European aristocracy (the Duke of Penaranda at El Guadalperal).

Both architects were, therefore, generally building for self-made adventurous men who, on the whole, respected their architects for their own successes. At Heathcote Mr Hemingway, a Yorkshire businessman, accepted the large estimate of £17,500 without question and also allowed the architect to furnish the house completely. This confidence even permitted Lutyens to ignore his client's requests for an oak staircase and build a black marble one which he knew his client did not want.[6] The resulting house was a great success for Lady Emily Lutyens wrote to her husband that friends near Ilkley had been asked '. . . if they knew Hemingway's house. "Know it" they said, "why it is the great sight of the neighbourhood. Even Americans come to see it" and they said how wise Hemingway was to have put himself entirely in your hands'.[7]

One of his chief sources of commissions was Edward Hudson, who had founded Country Life in 1897. He championed Lutyens and regularly published his houses in the magazine. Herbert Johnson saw Crooksbury in Country Life and sought its architect for Marshcourt. Mrs Belleville chose Lutyens for Papillon Hall in the same way and Julius Drewe approached Hudson to ask for suggestions of who he should use as the architect for his new castle in Devon. Apart from the publicity Hudson was a constant patron of Lutyens, asking him to build or modify a succession of houses for himself: Deanery Garden (1901), Lindisfarne Castle (1903), 15 Queen Anne's Gate (1906) and Plumpton Place (1927) as well as the construction of Country Life's own offices in Tavistock Street (1904).

Many commissions came through a network of friends in the city, in politics and through connections of his wife whose father, Lord Lytton, had been Viceroy in India. However, Lutyens had to work hard and was often a member of houseparties, tolerating the boredom of chasing clients or, in his own phrase, 'keeping them up to the mark'. Frequently he was exasperated when he was forgotten and jobs went to Aston Webb or Reginald Blomfield. However, Lutyens realised that what he wanted to build was expensive. In 1909 he wrote to his wife: 'I hate squalid houses and mean gardens—I want loveliness and cleanliness without conscious effort and that means help and help means money.'[8] In August 1909 he visited Sonning to see a Mr Buckley who wished to build a house, 'they are common and vulgar—motors and a launch in the river. Leading a life of absolute idleness punctuated by bridge and racing.'[9] In June 1912, 'I have to see a rich Parsee. He wants me to build him a house in Bombay. He is very rich so I shall see him, therefore, and if he looks tame, will spend money, etc. then it would be fun but if he looks difficult and won't spend money then I shall be polite and say "no" pleasantly.'[10] 'Lady Norman arrived, she is so difficult and wants impossibilities . . .

makes rooms larger than the site will hold and then wants to pack in anyhow essentials—an awful client and typical of all bureaucracy and vulgar minds.'[11] Occasionally he was depressed, 'I seem to have no real friends, just people I build for and then when the building is done I never see them again.'[12] But there is plenty of evidence in his correspondence of the friendships established with Hudson, the Farrers and the Barings as well as constant invitations to Folly Farm and Temple Dinsley.

Programme

The programme for the houses was very typical of the end of the nineteenth century. The development of the railways and the new accessibility gained meant greater choice in the location of sites. Owners could still be based in the city and there was less need of an estate to support a house. It also led to the idea of the country house weekend party with many visitors staying a comparatively short time and the requirement for more guest rooms as well as the lessening importance of stabling. Grey Walls at Gullane and Lindisfarne Castle are holiday homes without estates—the first related to the Muirfield Golf Links for a member of Parliament, the second a retreat on Holy Island for the editor of Country Life; both were distant from London but easily accessible. The Salutation at Sandwich is a small weekend retreat for a city banker in a country town built next to a gas works, which was reputed to be good for the asthmatic condition of its owner. Nashdom, a vast party house on a small site with very insignificant stables, acknowledges the importance of the railway line and station by proclaiming it a feature of the countryside in a childlike sketch on the painted wind-dial in the landing room.

Lutyens' houses generally have the same basic plan, generated by the requirements of the weekend house party and respecting the privacy and comfort of the guests through a hierarchic arrangement dividing the house between guests, family and staff. Thus an intercommunicating suite of reception rooms (consisting of a great room or hall supported on either side by a dining room and drawing room) a private retreat from guests (usually a library) and the kitchen accommodation are clearly separated. Linking these three elements, an independent hall/vestibule often appears as a transverse gallery parallel to the line of communication joining the three reception rooms. Frequently the gallery is repeated on the first floor. For functional reasons the kitchen wing adjoins the dining room and, because of orientation, the reception rooms are arranged to the south or west, leaving the north side for entry. The same plan is to be found in houses by Devey, such as St Albans Court, Nonington (1875), based on a similar programme.

Lutyens continued the nineteenth-century reaction of Nesfield and others against the formality of eighteenth-century life supported by rectangular rooms by designing rooms articulated into a series of sub-spaces using oriels, inglenooks and L-shaped rooms. Even in a house like Ednaston Manor the rectangular hall is divided into a series of five sub-spaces by the modulation of heavy ceiling beams in the low space.

Informality also produced the preference for the principal rooms to face south, again the reverse of the eighteenth century where they faced north to avoid the harmful effects of sunlight on both furnishings and occupants. For Lutyens, this influenced both the detail and planning of most houses. While the north and

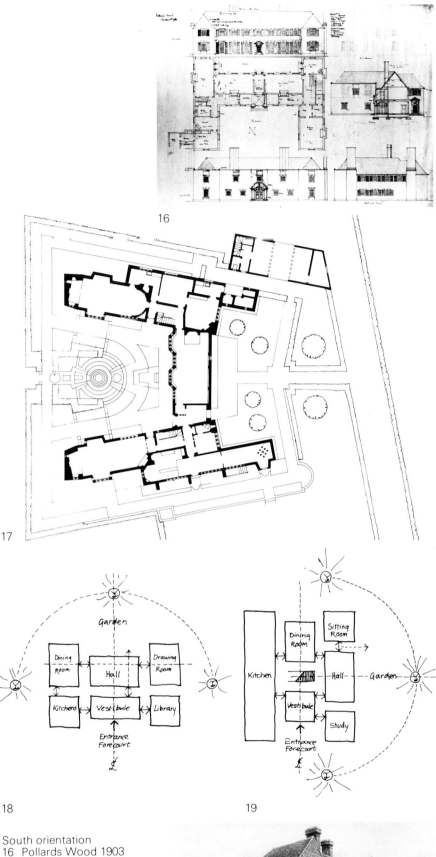

south elevations of Great Maytham are similar, the house was softened towards the garden by rows of apple-green shutters (now removed, sadly) and the extension of reception rooms out on to terraces related them to the garden and obliterated the basement storey, which disassociated the house from the north forecourt. At Pollards Wood and Gledstone Hall the same transformation of the façade occurs, but in both the house changes to the south with an alteration in the fenestration and with the roof becoming far more dominant. At Pollards Wood there is a change from a hip roof hidden behind a parapet on the north to one expressing its eaves on the south, but, as in several instances, this is not well resolved on the side elevation where the two systems meet.

Although Lutyens usually preferred a symmetrical form, such as a rectangular or H-plan approached from the north, the need to orientate the living rooms south-west and the resultant north-east service accommodation sometimes produced an asymmetrical bias in the plan, as at Marshcourt. Usually, however, difficult volumetric configurations were suppressed in the massing of the building by masking them with symmetrical elevations (Heathcote) or the problem was solved by treating the kitchens as a wing independent of the symmetrical mass of the main house (The Salutation) or hidden by screen walls (Castle Drogo). Another influence of orientation on the mass is seen at Goddards where the amount of south-facing wall is increased by the U-shaped west-facing court; the dining room and study which terminate the two wings both have more generous bay windows to the south side than the north and while the dining room looks out on to the court, the study turns away from it towards the sun ignoring the symmetrical organisation of the courtyard. However, this is not the case at Papillon Hall where the arrangement of the windows is determined by the symmetry of the Edwardian baroque 'butterfly' or 'suntrap' plan.

Where a north approach was impossible, Lutyens developed a variant of his basic plan. This is demonstrated by a group of four houses where symmetrical west fronts anticipate east-facing reception rooms beyond, but the plans are arranged to adjust to a south orientation by blocking the central axis within the building and redistributing the visitor from a second hall on the north-south axis approached from the entrance vestibule on the west-east axis. At Fulbrook House and Tigbourne Court the elevations acknowledge the turning of the axis, but at Homewood and The Salutation the importance of the east elevation is not supported by the plan. In all four, the second hall not only gives access to the reception rooms but also opens to the staircase so that the whole house including the first floor is independent of the entrance vestibule and organised with reference to the south front. While the floor plane of the reception rooms at The Salutation extends to terraces on the east and south fronts, nearly a quarter of the whole garden is raised as an artificial plane, level with the terrace on the south side. This lawn is enclosed as a quasi-internal volume by formal yew hedges and separated from the rest of the site by steps and brick gateways, acknowledging the importance of the preferred south orientation within the building. At Ednaston Manor the plan is basically of the Tigbourne type but the siting of the staircase beyond the entrance hall disengages the bedroom floor from the body of the house and the building loses much of the integrity achieved in the others.

To reinforce this point another example is the east

South orientation
16 Pollards Wood 1903 (BAL/RIBA)
17 Goddards 1899-1910 -plan of west-facing court
18 Diagram of relationship in Luytens, basic plan form
19 Variant adjusted to west-east approach
20 Fulbrook House 1897

21

approach to the Harriman House project, adjusted to the south in a very similar way but on a much larger scale. The visitor is led on the east-west axis to the heart of the building and redistributed by the Great Room on the cross axis which steps down to the group of reception rooms along the south front and again links in the Grand Staircase at its north end.

However, at Grey Walls and Papillon Hall the south approach would have completely compromised the privacy of the main rooms and their ideal orientation; in both Luytens set up a complex entry sequence to bring the visitor to the west side of the house so that the garden might be entered only from the house. At Grey Walls not only is the south garden screened by stone walls, but a second group of walls extends to enclose a complete, self-contained entrance court independent of the garden. The exaggeration of the entrance by the scale of the court itself and the diagonal geometry set up between the lodges and the curved entrance screen across the side of the house ensure that the house is used as the threshold to the south-facing garden. Similar results were achieved at Papillon: again the garden was screened and the entrance spaces given their own entity by exaggerated differentiation from the vernacular house. However, there it was classical detailing that led the visitor through a sequence of volumes from the portico embedded in the south-west corner of the house, across the circular basin court, to the vestibule on the west side of the building.

This problem was extended by the range of occupants using the buildings and led Lutyens to an equally complex array of entry devices which I shall now discuss. Typical solutions occur at Homewood, where the entrance porch cut deep into the house contains two front doors — for guests and service; at Nashdom, where a third category of party guests was dealt with by the division of the staircase within the main door, one leading to the big room, the other to the reception rooms; and at both Overstrand Hall and the Harriman House where discrete family entrances were provided in addition. Often the entrance porch also provides direct access to the garden (Munstead Wood, Papillon and Deanery Garden), although it is always subordinated to the entrance to the house so that the garden retains its privacy and remains an adjunct of the reception rooms.

The symmetrical arrangement of the west façade of Tigbourne Court, while acting in many ways as just a screen wall to the asymmetrical building behind it, is primarily to clarify the main entrance and provide a hierarchical framework for the kitchen and garden entrances as well as the service door. Each entrance has an independent forecourt formed by the shape of the building and by the use of different paving. While the plan of these forecourts is treated to appear almost like the drawing of a moulding, so that the parts are linked

22

23

24

25

Entrance
21 Grey Walls 1900
22 Papillon Hall 1903 (CL c.1910)
23 Tigbourne Court 1899 -a symmetrical entrance screen to an assymmetrical house (CL 1905)
24 Abbotswood 1901 -the square forecourt created by classical detailing (obliterated in a recent remodelling) (CL 1913)
25 Barton St Mary 1906 -the unbuilt entrance vestibule (Weaver 1913)

26

27

Typical of the views published in *Country Life,* the photograph taken in 1913 (26) of the remodelling, by Lutyens of the west front at Abbotswood belies the scale of the building which is revealed by the south front of the original Victorian house (27) photographed in 1979

together, symmetry and scale subordinate the kitchen and garden entrances. The main entrance is also emphasised by surface articulation, dressed stone classical details as opposed to coursed rubble and by the contrast of the horizontal entrance loggia with the verticality of the gateways. The recession of the loggia below the flat plane of the three-gabled wall above it gives the appearance that the mass of the house has been cut to reveal the crisp red-brick walls within and access to the building has already been made once the forecourt has been entered; this is echoed by the red-tile voussoirs around the secondary entrances but their treatment stresses the wall surface rather than revealing the interior.

The main entrance to Abbotswood, a Victorian vernacular house which Lutyens altered in 1901, is equally exaggerated to give it predominance. The vestibule is entered from a square forecourt created by four rusticated piers with freestanding pineapple finials independent of the front of the building. Lutyens used the axiality of the square's co-ordinates to locate the entrance to what is in effect a free-form house. The doorway however, again because of its classical

detailing, belongs not to the order of the house but to the square court which acts as the real entrance to the building and the vast three-storey rustic gable Lutyens laid across the corner of the existing house is established by the width of the court and brings together the elements of the existing house and the entrance court.

Several thresholds are arranged to reassure the visitor and provide a feeling of security on entering Lutyens' houses. Often the point of welcome is well within the body of the building and the house is made independent of the entry sequence which is experienced only on arrival. At Tigbourne and Homewood the forecourt, porch and vestibule are crossed before arrival in the hall in the centre of the south front. Each area is articulated by means of paving, steps, pilasters and beams as a series of sub-spaces to increase the sense of the progression; the hall is eventually reached, set away from the vestibule, across a subordinate space. As already mentioned the organisation of the house is then independent and, with the balancing arrangement of the vestibule and dining room doors either side of the staircase arch, the entrance vestibule becomes insignificant to the life within the house. Equally the forecourt, porch and vestibule are given their own independence as separate entities linked by the main axis and disengaged from the hall by the interuption of the axis and a minor doorway.

This independence of the house from the entry vestibule is stressed at Barton St Mary, East Grinstead, where the vestibule, like Abbotswood, is actually an 'unbuilt' volume; in this case a square courtyard sunk below the level of the drive and garden. The point of entry to the house is declared on the main axis at the circular steps leading into this space, but the axis is blocked at the hall and a minor door and lobby set to one side emphatically disengage the house from its 'entrance'. In both examples the arrival sequence is treated as an important gesture and then set away from the activity of the house.

Enlargement
There is in nearly every house evidence of Lutyens' attempts to increase the apparent size of the building. This occurs not only in the detailed planning but also in the way he organised visitors' movement through the house. The size is also increased by the external massing and above all by the relationship of house to garden, which was often considered an integral extension of the house itself rather than ancillary to it.

Many of the photographs here were taken by Charles Latham of *Country Life* soon after the completion of the individual houses and it can be assumed that they are images of the buildings approved by the architect. Even in these we see an exaggeration of scale because the photographs were frequently taken with an eye level only a couple of feet above ground. The west front of Tigbourne in Latham's photograph not only increased the size of the house by exaggerating the height of the single-storey drawing room wing in comparison with the three-storey body of the house beyond, but also implied a far greater geometric control of the whole than exists in reality and in some respects conceals a rather small-scale 'arts and crafts' villa.

Within the house the separation of the building into constituent parts for entry, guests, family and servants in response to the programme increases the building's apparent volume because of the isolation of these elements from each other. Enlargement also occurs in detail planning. The use of Colin Campbell's device at Houghton House (1735) of setting arches either side of the dining room fireplace to include the servery space behind the fireplace within the room increases the volume of the dining rooms at Gledstone, Middleton and El Guadalperal. The diagonal shift of axis across the vestibule, hall and dining room gives an unexpected dimension to Ednaston Manor.

The discovery of unanticipated volumes is another instance. At Ednaston the small first-floor windows conceal the inversion of the scale of the ground and first floors and the low reception rooms contrast with the bedrooms extended by coved ceilings up into the roof space. At The Salutation neither the elevations nor ground-floor plan reveal that a third of the whole building's volume is taken up by a more than generous staircase of Italian inspiration rising in stages between walls around an enigmatic void. The generosity of the stair and landings is only revealed as the visitor moves up through the small house.

Lutyens often expresses a sequence of rooms opening into each other to increase the scale of the building. At Deanery Garden the three reception rooms are linked by double doors on a cross axis, extending from the dining room fireplace to the sitting room bay window; the double-height hall on the principal axis of the house unites the three about the oriel window by subordinating the single-height supporting volumes. While five reception rooms at Nashdom are similarly linked together about a small, double-height winter garden, the constant variation in the shapes and volumes of the rooms conflicts with the hierarchy that unifies Deanery Garden and makes them appear purely as transitional spaces which fail as drawing room, dining room and smoking room.

In some cases, where the house is a conversion of an existing building and the basic plan could not be employed, the reception rooms are dispersed about the house. At Whalton Manor Lutyens enlarged the visitor's experience of the building by treating the connecting rooms and staircases as a virtually processional route. Castle Drogo must also be considered in this category as Lutyens' brief was so drastically reduced, a year after construction had started in 1911, that the house had to be an adaptation of existing work. The complexity of its circulation spaces, articulated by arches, domes, windows and flights of steps to control movement through them to the reception rooms distributed on three levels, is so theatrical that the rooms themselves prove an anticlimax. After the Great War the design was further compromised and single-storey reception rooms were substituted for the intended double-height volumes.[13]

Frequently Lutyens encouraged movement backwards and forwards within the building so that the architectural experience would be more extensive than the house would otherwise allow. Through axial planning he reinforced the importance of certain rooms, but direct access was denied by the interruption of movement on axis and the visitor was drawn across the transverse spaces of the house and back again. Heathcote's arrangement, combining the basic Lutyens' plan with the development of the variant used later at The Salutation, is a prime example of this. The symmetrical mass of the house is approached from the north and entered on the main axis which extends through the hall and out into the garden on the south side. The entrance vestibule, however, is off axis and the visitor enters towards one end. Movement on axis is

28

29

30

Enlargement
28 Gledstone Hall 1922-25. The servery included within the dining room (CL 1935)
29 Deanery Garden 1901. The hall unites a sequence of three reception rooms (CL c.1905)
30 Castle Drogo 1910-30. Dining room staircase (CL 1945)

Opposite
31 Gledstone Hall 1922-25, south front
32 Overstrand Hall 1899-1901, south and east fronts
33 Orchards 1897-99, looking back across the gardens to the north front

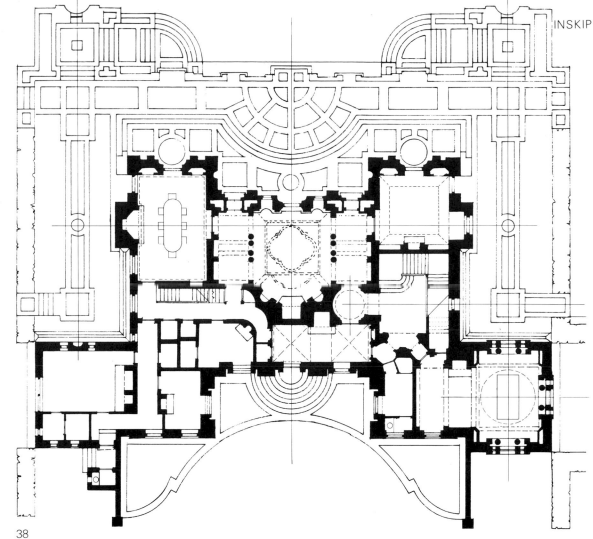

38

39

interrupted by being blocked by the back of the hall fireplace and the visitor is turned to the right. This is partially achieved by the repetition to the west of the groin vault, by the brick panels inset in the floor and by the symmetrical arrangement of the vestibule itself about its fireplace. This establishes a diagonal symmetry which relates the entrance doors to those leading to the hall lobby to the right of the vestibule fireplace.

The lobby includes views of the staircase hall into the entry sequence and leads to a subordinate space at the side of the great hall, in effect a mediaeval screens passage. Again the pattern of the marble floor and plaster vault pull the visitor past the first arch that could lead into the hall towards the external wall and the doors leading to the terrace. The gradual increase in both light and volume from the vestibule, the height of which is ambiguously suggested at the top of the stone panelling, to the hall, which extends up displacing the bedroom above it, as well as the symmetrical repetition of the screens passage across the other side of the room, attracts the visitor towards the major space seen through the tight intercolumniation of the screen. The cross axis linking the drawing room and dining room through the hall (as at Deanery Garden) turns the visitor into the room and the change of the floor finish to oak boards acknowledges entry. The expression of the thick external wall by the depth of the window embrasures detaches the room from the exterior and movement turns back on the principal north-south axis and terminates at the fireplace set in the apsidal wall backing on to the vestibule.

The basic plan type used by Lutyens also enlarged the

houses, producing a preference for narrow buildings determined by the width of one reception room plus the circulation space. This increased the size of the house externally and led to an extravagant amount of external wall and roof surface in relationship to the enclosed volume. In addition to this Lutyens incorporated courtyards within his buildings whenever possible because of the additional volume and mass they gave a house. In small works, like Munstead Wood or Deanery Garden, the court could only be U-shaped because of the restricted amount of accommodation. Because of the single rooms planned around them, they are seldom important as light wells and, while the court at Tigbourne is used as an entry court, the circulation to Deanery Garden and Nashdom is peripheral to the courtyard, which has little apparent use. Orchards is of the basic planning type placed on the far side of an entrance court protected by a gateway after Shaw's model at Leyswood. Certain elements are stretched out to enclose the court: the service accommodation is adjusted to form the east side and the 'private retreat', in this case Lady Chance's studio, is removed from the usual position to one beside the west gate and connected to the rest of the house by an open cloister which alone forms the south side of the court.

While the courtyard at Overstrand Hall enlarges the building and allows a very rich entry experience (the axial approach to the entrance gate is subordinated to the axis of the courtyard and passes down one side of the court until the fountain basin acts as a rotation point that takes the visitor up curved steps to the front door on the central axis) it disengages the principal rooms on the south side of the court from the dining room and service accommodation to the north and, again, circulation space is used to complete the courtyard.

However, in large projects such as the Harriman House there is enough accommodation for the court to be contained within the house; El Guadalperal demonstrates that the plans for Lutyens' larger houses tend to be much simpler in terms of movement through them as they do not require devices to enlarge the architectural experience and the courtyard is used to link a series of elements—the Duke's wing, the main reception rooms, the King's wing, the Chapel court and the Kitchen court.

Additional volumes are often included by implication: Tigbourne Court is enlarged by the completion of the negative volumes delineated by the concave wings either side of the forecourt, not only from the road but from the terrace where the height of the convex wall implies the containment of an enclosed volume beyond the drawing room. Whereas only half of the rectangular courtyard at Marshcourt is contained by buildings the remainder of the enclosure is so clearly defined that the dry moat and bridge, which echo the house in their detailing, imply the missing volumes and gatehouse and in this light the plan becomes identical to that of Orchards. Similarly, the partial demolition of Castle Drogo, implied by its fragmentary quality, enlarges the house not only back to the basic Lutyens' plan but makes it appear as the U-shaped building around the court that was originally intended.[13]

The site

Turning now to the relationship between house and garden, which I have already hinted at, it can be seen that this is clearly of paramount importance to Lutyens' architecture. Either the geometric structure of the house is extended to the whole site or garden elements are treated as fictive fortifications protecting the

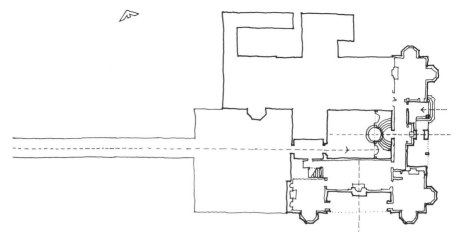

40

41

42

Enlargement
40 Overstrand hall 1899
41 Tigbourne Court 1899 -an assembly of actual and implied volumes (CL 1905)
42 Castle Drogo 1910-30 - the symmetrical design is completed by implication

terraces from the surrounding countryside. In both ways the unity of house and garden is established. Two reasons become apparent for this: first, the desire to enlarge the experience of the house into something much larger than could be reasonably expected and second, the wish to preserve the ethos of a special place. Many of the ideas controlling the interior apply to the garden, but it must, of course, be noted that while the structuring of the gardens appears similar to the house in plan, with the implication of enclosed room or gallery-like volumes, the volumetric control is different because it is formed only by terracing the site, planting, low walls, water courses and carefully placed sculptural elements.[14] The treatment of Lambay Castle provides an introductory example.

In 1910, while still working on the castle whose

The Site
43 Lambay Castle 1908. Looking back along the approach (CL 1929)
44 Lambay - a horizontal plane implied over the garden courts
45 The Red House, Effingham, 1892 (BAL/RIBA)
46 Little Thakeham 1902 -the private drive treated as a country lane (CL 1909)
47 Goddards 1910 - yew hedges as fictive fortifications

43   44

45

46

47

restoration he had started in 1905, he wrote to his wife: *'I was impounded on Lambay. The castle is pretty as well but the weather has been bad and getting material to the place well nigh impossible. I do wish you could come to Lambay. It is such a delicious aloof place alone in its wash of waters.'*[15]

The approach to Lambay is controlled to stress the remoteness of the castle on its island off the Dublin coast. To support this, Lutyens placed the whole castle complex within a circular rampart enclosure to harbour it from the surrounding bleak sea of grass analagous to the Irish Channel—an island within an island. Today there is not even a track denoting the approach uphill across the field to the rampart. The entrance gate, gridded to appear like a portcullis, is set between two primitive stone bastions whose ruggedness seems timeless and leads to the security of the haven, with the ramparts protecting not only the extended castle but also Lutyens' new garden, farm buildings and orchards from the hostile world.

The circular enclosure itself is in turn anchored back into the hillside by tangential plantations and an axial radiating avenue. From the rough grass the route changes within this refuge to a lawn path edged with flagstones running through an avenue to the gate of the west forecourt. At either end the flagstones return in an arc across the path so that it becomes a finite element like a drawbridge lowered across the plantation from the gate of the forecourt to the gate in the rampart. A second gridded screen, but now set between classical piers in garden walls, leads to the west forecourt. When the route enters the forecourt the lawn path becomes paved and is checked first by a narrow rill and then by a cross axis before reaching the castle. The wildness of the island is tamed by the formal devices of the court and the transitions allow civilisation to exist by stressing rather than destroying the romantic quality of the place.

The courts immediately around the house are so closely allied with it that they become part of the built form; a datum is established at the top of the walls around the north and west courts, common with the edge of the north lawn steps, and implies a horizontal plane covering the courts linking them with the house. In this way the house is enlarged on the immediate scale then extended by routes and geometrically controlled planting along its axes to the circular rampart to enclose its own microcosm. At the same time as this enlargement the apparent mass of the original castle is not compromised by the new kitchen court for the addition is disengaged diagonally and suppressed into the hillside under a hip roof so that the original keep still dominates the whole.

The seeds of this idea of the house's alliance with its immediate site and the distancing of the surroundings are found in Lutyens' early works. The sketch for a house at Effingham shows the wings common with the garden walls incorporating the court with the house and excluding the outside world; at Little Thakeham the forecourt is similarly integrated and the private drive outside is treated merely as a country lane passing the building. At Goddards the garden court is included within the body of the house; the lawns remain remote from the house, which is surrounded by clipped yew hedges which form fictive fortifications.

Orchards is protected from its almost suburban approach by two courts. One implied by the stable building whose buttresses modulate the drive outside the courtyard gateway and the actual court around which the house is grouped. The sides of the gateway are canted in plan to control the drive by reducing its width and the court is further protected by large barn-like timber gates. This security is supported to the east where a series of enclosed gardens and terraces stretch out from the loggia towards the view across the valley. Through their geometric form and materials these are associated with the house and contrasted with the countryside; the whole is contained on the east by a raised 'wall walk' similar to the rampart at Lambay. However, the idea is not borne out to the south where the house merges with its surroundings and there is so little definition between the garden and the countryside that the lack of 'defences' on this side reduces the validity of the fortified entrance and terraces.

On the other hand, Deanery Garden of 1901 demonstrates the fully fledged idea. The site of the house was an ancient brick-walled orchard and Lutyens divided it so that a series of spaces was allied with the house and grouped together to overlook the remaining orchard. The house is placed against the north wall of the site and encloses a court within the building similar to the Effingham sketch. A principal axis (extending from the entrance into the orchard) unifies the house and garden, but this is interrupted by a flight of semi-circular steps set in a retaining wall which differentiates areas to the north and south and associates them with the house or orchard. Three parallel axes relate the gardens to the interior of the house and unify the north end of the site by crossing the main axis. The shift across the site caused by their increasing length from the common base of the pergola, which defines the west edge of the terrace, is sympathetic to the shift from the entrance to the central axis of the building's mass, which we have seen unites the internal spaces about the oriel window. The orthogonal arrangement of these axes also contrasts the terraces with the diagonal cross routes of the orchard. Within the areas allied with the building Lutyens establishes a hierarchy of spaces that culminate with the great hall of the house.

Although the house is extended on three sides by terraces, each terrace is independent of the others, joined only by gateways or steps and, even if it runs beyond the extent of the building, relating only to one face of the house rather than joining to become a continuous garden surrounding the building. The entrance route divides the terraces into sections either side of it and the division is reinforced by a change in level along the west side of the path giving the upper terrace a dominance over the lower. The upper terrace repeats the plan of the house, shifted diagonally across the axis, and the house and terrace are both anchored to the site horizontally by their common floor plane and vertically by the massive brick chimney beside the garden doorway. The side of the chimney-stack is splayed diagonally in plan so as to serve as a reference plane relating the terrace through to the hall inside the house at the same time as the oriel window is tightly gridded to preserve the strength of the wall surface and remove the hall from the lower terrace which it overlooks.

Lutyens supported the idea of a fortified site with romantic references which, indeed, treat the house as a metaphoric castle. While the lower terrace is considered as a dry moat separating the house from the orchard, the upper terrace is a bridge extending out from the house to link the two elements. The rill running along the base of the moat reinforces these ideas by rising in a cicular pool that has to be bridged by the upper terrace; its exotic quality recalls the thirteenth-century

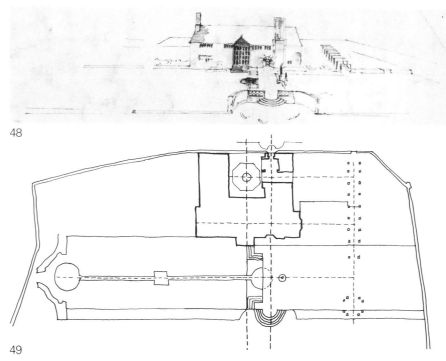

48

49

Generalife at Granada to contrast with the mediaeval pastoral of the orchard and the water contained in the narrow channel is treated as something very precious, to be stored in tanks and raised by elaborate handpumps, almost in anticipation of a siege. The semi-circular steps leading from the orchard to the terrace are emphasised to act as a gatehouse and stress that the house is raised above the surroundings. This is supported further by Gertrude Jekyll's planting scheme: while old roses clamber through the orchard trees, and much of Lutyens' geometry is softened by indigenous plants, the terraces contrast with the surroundings by the introduction of exotics, the use of tubs of plants and topiary yews; even the pergola extends to a rose arbour to provide a lookout post commanding the orchard.

The delineated boundary

Given that Lutyens' houses are enlarged by the use of external spaces allied to the building, often used as 'fortifications' against the surroundings, a delineated line marking the boundary is always apparent even if its position varies in relationship to the house. Deanery Garden subdivided a small contained site so that one part could be disassociated and overlooked from the other allied with the building. Nashdom repeats the arrangement at Deanery Garden, but at Heathcote the house extends to include the whole site and it is the suburban surroundings outside that are distanced. The classical style of Heathcote and the formality of its supporting terraces were chosen to set the house apart from the 'villadom' on the edge of Ilkley in which it is located. The house and garden are unified with an apsidal theme extending from the great lawn to the hall so that the whole forms a pyramidal composition contrasting with the neighbouring houses. Similarly, the whole site at Grey Walls is united with the house and set apart from its suburban context by a series of formal courtyard enclosures, interlocked together in plan. Their stone walls and grey-pantile coping extend the materials of the house throughout the site. The whole acts as a low pyramidal composition which steps up across the elevations of the house and as at Lombay the constant height of the garden walls establishes a datum, implying a horizontal plane covering both the entrance and garden courts.

Deanery Garden 1901
48 Conceptual sketch
   c.1899 (BAL/RIBA)
49 Analytical plan

In all these examples, as already noted at Deanery Garden, the spaces allied to the house are an independent series of enclosures and relate only to one façade, rather than forming a continuous garden in which the house sits. It becomes apparent, at Heathcote and Grey Walls, that this was used to increase the contrast with the context from which Lutyens' houses are separated and that the context was always considered as a continuous surround to the whole. This is also shown in the treatment of large-scale houses set in their own parkland and in cases where Lutyens was concerned with actual rather than metaphoric castles.

At Ednaston, while the house is supported by entrance courts and terraces, it is the private parkland that is distanced. A walled forecourt disengages the entrance front from the three radiating horse chestnut avenues in the park. The separation is stressed by turning the niched gatepiers towards the drive so that an independent space exists between the two parts; the south terrace is raised above the park and removed from it by a sheer drop rather than by a ha-ha, a device seldom used by Lutyens, and the east garden is completely self-contained by its terracing and enclosed by brick walls, yew hedges and trees. Gledstone Hall is as isolated from its park as Heathcote is from its surroundings and the house is experienced as bounded by the circular lawn in the forecourt, the circular pool terminating the canal.

The porticoed entrance is protected by two forecourts and the garden contained within bastion-like stone walls with a pergola across the south end. The geometric terracing of the garden sharply contrasts with the undulating park and the artificiality of the horizontal terraces is stressed by the reflecting canal whose water is set almost flush with the surrounding stonework.

While the remote quality of the original castle on Lambay could have been lost, the addition of the all-encompassing rampart enlarged the castle from the building itself to the whole enclosure and preserved its defensive position on the island. However, it is the rock at Lindisfarne and the promontory at Castle Drogo which provide their protection. Because of this any external spaces required were included within the body of the house in the form of ramparts or roof terraces and the gardens were removed from the immediate vicinity. Outside the castle was directly surrounded by the distanced site. At Lindisfarne, Lutyens' restoration alternately incorporated external and internal spaces as the visitor moved up though the building. The flower garden, an independent rectangular stone enclosure, is sited away across a field so as not to compromise the castle's isolation set as it is among ornamental highland cattle.

While Lambay and Lindisfarne are both conversions of sixteenth-century shells, Castle Drogo was a new building. Again, so that the promontory could be the fortification, the gardens are removed a short walk from the house and the sequence of enclosures that culminates in a circular lawn surrounded by a yew hedge are screened from the building.[16] However, with the reduction from a courtyard scheme the definition of the entrance forecourt was insufficient for the intended protection of the building when approached from the north drive. Lutyens attempted to correct this but his proposals never progressed beyond the construction of a full-scale timber and canvas mock-up of a castellated gateway which would have re-established the lost courtyard. He finally had to resort to using wall-like yew hedges, which fail in their purpose although they appear convincing in plan.

Not only with the castles and their ramparts but in every case the idea of the protective enclosures is supported by a lookout which reinforces containment by a release. The pergola at Deanery Garden and the Thunder House at Munstead Wood both provide a position from which one may overlook one's surroundings in 'safety'. The south terrace at Ednaston and the great terrace at the head of the steps at Nashdom act as promenades commanding the rest of the site; a gazebo on the central axis of the private gardens at Grey Walls both frames the view of the country beyond and re-establishes the containment of the garden walls which have reduced their heights on either side. Looking from the house the canal at Gledstone terminates with a view to the distant horizon through a divided pergola, but on reaching the pergola an avenue of apple trees and a gardener's cottage are found on the central axis concealed at a lower level by the sloping site, the discovery of which stresses the removal of the terraced enclosure from the landscape.

The delineated boundary
50 Gledstone Hall - isolated from its park (CL 1935)
51 Lindisfarne Castle - the walled garden
52 Castle Drogo - full-scale mock-up of unexecuted castellated gateway and screen walls c.1913 (Anthony Drewe collection)
53 Gledstone Hall - section: containment supported by a release

50

51

52

53

The idea of climax

As shown with the example of Deanery Garden, there is an hierarchic arrangement of spaces within the protected area very similar to that of a mediaeval castle organised about its keep. In most of the early houses the hall was dominant but, after the use of the external court as the principal volume of Goddards (1899-1910) and the upper and lower batteries that dominate the internal spaces at Lindisfarne, Lutyens gradually moved towards using the garden terrace as the climax around which his houses were organised. This is especially true with his more frequent use of the classical style. The development is seen in four houses: Little Thakeham (1902), Heathcote (1905), Great Maytham (1907) and Gledstone Hall (1922). Each is planned symmetrically about a main north-south axis with an identical linear sequence of independent spaces arranged along the axis: forecourt, entrance vestibule, hall and garden.

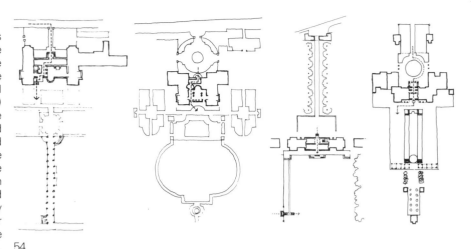

54

55

56

Little Thakeham and Heathcote show a move towards making the hall the climax of the whole site, rather than of just a house, while Great Maytham and Gledstone show the change to the use of the garden as the dominant element.

In both Little Thakeham and Heathcote the hall is emphasised by its increased height as the climax of a group of three reception rooms. It is disengaged from the exterior, only indirectly connected to the terrace via a screens passage, and the reception rooms are bounded on the cross axis by fireplaces and chimney-stacks at the house's extremities. In both, movement on axis is blocked in the vestibule by the wall of the hall so that it has to be entered off axis from the screens passage. I have already suggested that Lutyens interrupted movement on the main axis for two reasons: to readjust his houses to a south orientation and to increase their apparent sizes by introducing complicated circulation patterns. We how now have a third reason — the same device is used to divide the house into areas associated with the forecourt and with the garden, the wall blocking the axis being the demarcation between the two. At Little Thakeham the hall is clearly related to the garden by its oriel window and by the exaggerated distance of the room from the entrance. However, it is still independent of the garden because the emphasis of the room is moved to the east of the main axis about the fireplace which is offset opposite a virtually windowless wall rather than related to the oriel. At Heathcote, the hall is located firmly on axis and the garden becomes far more involved with the interior. The pyramidal composition heralds the house as the climax of the terraced site and terminates within the building at the fireplace set in the apsidal wall of the hall backing on to the vestibule. Heathcote can be

57

The garden as climax
54 Plans illustrating the transition from using the hall to using the garden as the principal volume of the house
Little Thakeham 1902
Heathcote 1906
Great Maytham 1907-09
Gledstone 1922-25
55 Goddards 1899 (CL)
56 Little Thakeham 1902 -the double-height hall set asymmetrically in the house is contained behind a virtually blank façade (CL 1909)
57 Gledstone 1922-25

considered as a series of chinese boxes one set within another — the hall is the final goal.

At neither Great Maytham nor Gledstone is the hall stressed by a volumetric increase and in both remains a single-height space. The main axis is no longer interrupted within the house and the visitor allowed to pass on axis from the vestibule through the hall out to the garden. French doors open from the reception rooms directly on to the terraces rather than via separate lobbies, fireplaces are moved to internal walls so that chimney-stacks no longer mark the boundaries of the house and views are permitted on the cross axis. Thus the house becomes an introductory pavilion supporting the gardens; a development of Lutyens' idea of the house as a threshold to the garden even though in the early houses the garden was subordinate to the house.

It is ambiguous as to whether the house or the garden is the climax at Great Maytham: on the one hand the building is elevated on a basement storey to command the garden, but on the other the strength of the route from gatehouse, down the avenue, across the forecourt, through the house to the great lawn is such that it passes straight through the house making the hall insignificant in comparison with the garden beyond. However, the great lawn, which is only defined by its horizontal surface and marked by the existing brick garden wall to the west, is totally open to the south and proves an anti-climax. It fails to contain movement on the axis through its lack of definition and becomes yet another incident on a continuous route.

Gledstone repeats the pattern of Great Maytham but is adjusted so that the terraced garden becomes the climax. Lutyens united the house and garden by setting them on one horizontal level which contrasts with the undulating park. This plane extends throughout the areas allied to the building; the forecourt is cut into the ground and continues as a raised plane through the house, out across the terraces to the south pergola, by which time the ground beyond has dropped a whole storey in height. He also reduced the importance of the house in relation to the garden; the building itself sits directly on the horizontal plane rather than being raised on a terrace and is suppressed under a large hip roof; the pergola implies a repetition of the mass of the house at the south end of the garden and symmetry subordinates the two built forms as pavilions about the central canal, recessed as a separate garden into the plane of the terrace.

The circular pool set within the divided pergola equates with the hall set within the house; the controlled view over the south pool to the distant countryside parallels the view through the house to the north forecourt and park and the gardener's cottage recalls the lodges. While the Ionic portico of the house is the entrance gate to the garden, the hall is supported by subsidiary spaces on the main axis formed by a columnar screen which disengages the vestibule and a space between a pair of Loggias disengages the garden. In some respects these reinstate the blocking of the axis either side of the hall seen at Heathcote but they allow movement on axis and permit the hall to be subordinated to, rather than dominated by, the garden beyond.

Paradox

While several of Lutyens' houses suffer from pomposity and predictability because of their programme and the use of a basic planning approach, the best houses avoid this through the use of paradox: much of the enjoyment of these houses largely depends on the contradiction of an idea established within the design. There are frequent instances throughout Nashdom, which appears to be entered axially through the portico and across an external courtyard. But the entrance is to one side of the portico, the route is peripheral to the court and the main axis is not regained until arrival in the winter garden on the south front. The terracing of the steeply sloping site is concealed from the road and masked by the house which appears a five-storey structure from the drive but only three-storey from the garden. The terrace at right angles to the house marks the side of a peaceful, square lawn in front of the intimate south elevation, but its monumental staircases exaggerate the drama of the change in level within the garden. The continuity of the south façade suggests the house is a single mass, but above the parapet level it is actually separated into two pavilions through the arrangement of chimney-stacks which cut back to allow a sky light over the winter garden concealed by the cartouche.

The last contradiction is reinforced by the unexpected transparency of the centre of the house back across the court to the lane and the treatment of the winter garden as a quasi-external space continues the division of the house by a series of external spaces inserted into its mass — the loggia, court and winter garden — and interrupts the linear sequence of reception rooms. Contradiction is also apparent in the details: the austerity that gradually appears in the evolution of the house's design, moving away from the preliminary grandiose detailing, is hardly in the opulent spirit of the parties for which the building was intended and attempts to deflate the pretentiousness of some of Princess Dolgorouki's French furniture. The white-washed brickwork contrasts with the sophistication of the Tuscan portico's detailing and the simplicity of the elevations, relieved only by apple-green shutters, is juxtaposed with the richness of the red-brick chimney-stacks, with their stone dressings, that rise from the tiled roof. The grandeur of the wide Italian-type stair rising in a straight run from the entrance door is supported by being placed under a constant ceiling level but questioned by the low ceiling height at the head of the stair. The unpretentiousness of the stables is stressed by the insertion of a giant Tuscan order at the entrance arch.

The concealed accommodation of additional facilities often contradicts the general arrangement of the building but their revelation increases the visitor's enjoyment. The south elevation at Nashdom conceals that the double-height winter garden only rises through the central bay and that the additional height of the big room is gained by raising the floor of the bedrooms

Nashdom 1905-09
58 The terracing of the site concealed from the house
59 The Big Room - the unexpected inclusion of the organ gallery above the entrance door (CL 1912

58

59

60

61

above. However, in neither case does the fenestration respond to these changes. While the descent from the big room to the entrance is not shown on the external elevation and the windows remain at a constant level relating to the floor of the reception rooms, the low ceiling over the head of the stair accommodates an extra storey to form an organ gallery overlooking the big room and this is declared on the elevation by a row of *oeil de boeuf* windows.

Interior decoration

Lutyens' approach to interior decoration employed the idea he discovered in looking at vernacular buildings of contrasting the grand and humble; he often used farmhouse furniture within a more sophisticated context. Frequently the austerity of the furnishings was an essential deflating architectural element to balance the grandeur of some details. The 'spartan life' intended for the Barings at Lambay and Hudson at Lindisfarne was supported by whitewashed walls and oak floors painted duck-egg blue or crimson with a thin coat of white paint dragged over. The furniture was seventeenth-century oak, mainly stripped of all polish and bleached, and simple eighteenth-century rush-seated ladder-back chairs supplemented with the occasional piece in the same manner designed by the architect. Groups of seventeenth-century portrait engravings such as Lombart's 'Countesses' framed in painted bolection or antique Hogarth mouldings hung on the walls with chintz curtains on hinged curtain poles housed in the window reveals. He applied this image to most of his early houses, derived largely from the way Gertrude Jekyll furnished Munstead Wood with her mania for collecting country furniture and from John Ruskin's dictum to her that *'good whitewashed timber and tapestry are the proper walls of rooms in cold climates'.*[17]

At Castle Drogo Lutyens designed all the kitchen furniture in scrubbed oak as an essential part of the design of the service spaces, but he was not involved with the furnishing of the house and much of the furniture there is mediocre or pretentious, purchased by Julius Drewe lock, stock and barrel with a previous house in Sussex. Lutyens' decoration survived at Lindisfarne until recently when unfortunately the house was rearranged by the National Trust and the oak floors stripped of their paintwork and polished. The interiors of many houses such as Munstead Wood and Little Thakeham have lost much of their meaning with the introduction of suburban furnishings — perhaps it is Lutyens' fault, decoration is too ephemeral to be used as a primary architectural element.

Lutyens' use of contrast was comensurate with his frequent use of black in decoration.[18] He believed that mouldings should be painted white so that light could bring out the detail and set off by black coves, as at Whalton. Occasionally a slight ambiguity is established through the use of black; it is difficult to ascertain the exact relationship of the dome to its cornice in the vestibule at The Salutation. The use of black led to *'great dignity in decoration'* and was *'conducive to magnificence'.*[19] At 29, Bloomsbury Square his own drawing room had black walls with white woodwork, relieved by a green/white drag-painted floor and adjoining a red dining room. When the Lutyenses moved to Bedford Square the black scheme was repeated for the drawing room but approached from a staircase lined with silver paper with a vermilion skirting. At Folly Farm, Venetian-red balconies introduced a minor incidence of colour to the hall with its matt-black walls.

With the increasing sophistication of the classical

Vernacular Furnishing
60 Deanery Garden 1901 - Lutyens ladderback dining chairs and sideboard recall eighteenth-century farmhouse prototypes (CL c.1905)
61 Munstead Wood - the hall: whitewash and oak (CL 1900)

Black and White
62 Folly Farm 1906 - The Hall: black and white with grey carpet, the balconies red (CL c.1910)
63 Homewood 1901 - The Hall (CL c.1905)
64 Gledstone 1922-25. Alternating black and white marble treads (CL 1935)

62

63

64

Le Bois des Moutiers, Varangeville-sur-Mer, France ▶
1898, garden front. Lutyens retained the substance
of this nineteenth-century Normandy villa but made
many alterations

Le Bois des Moutiers, entrance front. Lutyens added
the staircase and great chimney

65

66

Faked History
65 Munstead Wood 1896 -'does not stare with newness' (CL 1900)
66 St Alban's Court, Nonnington, 1875-78, by George Devey (CL)

houses and the greater unity of all their parts, Lutyens moved away from vernacular furniture and materials to eighteenth-century polished pieces and more colour appeared in the decoration. A cloudy green front door led to the entrance vestibule at Heathcote where red-brick herringbone panels decorated the stone floor and a sky-blue vault surmounted the stone panelling. The white-painted hall was relieved by a *fleur de pêche* chimney-piece and green Siberian marble columns and the staircase hall lined with cream Ancaster stone had a brilliant green carpet running up the black marble treads. Usually, colour was limited to the natural material or restricted to accessories.

However, Lutyens' preference for *'bareness and whiteness'* and his avoidance of applied pattern prevailed at Gledstone where a white scheme was highlighted by bands of black in the picture rail, dado and skirting which run throughout the ground floor. The alternating black and white marble treads of the staircase, that look so good but can prove so lethal, while continuing the dado rail across the stair were contained under the black cove of the ceiling above.[20]

'Archaeology'

The use of antique furniture was intended to produce an illusion of age, especially when bleached and scrubbed. Buildings themselves were often treated in a similar way and materials chosen for quick-weathering properties. At Munstead Wood some of the oak was limed and sand blasted and the stone of Little Thakeham gives the appearance of three centuries of wear. For Lutyens *'the visible result of time is a large factor in realised aesthetic value'* and objections by his contemporaries such as Sir Robert Lorimer, who cristicised Munstead Wood for its induced antiquity, were ignored.

Lutyens' 'archaeological' attitude was crucial to his design approach on two counts. Firstly, as Robert Lutyens pointed out in his biography of his father,[21] there were two very conservative influences in his life; the vernacular tradition represented by his upbringing at Thursley in Surrey and the aristocratic tradition of his wife's family at Knebworth House in Hertfordshire. Both stressed the importance of continuity. Lutyens, disturbed by the way society was changing, sought refuge in traditional values and became self-consciously anachronistic. Secondly, he worked largely for *nouveau riche* clients who, following the nineteenth-century pattern, sought historical styles for the security they offered. On the one hand Gertrude Jekyll was, therefore, delighted that Munstead *'. . . does not stare with newness; it is not new in any way that is disquieting to the eye; it is neither raw nor callow. On the contrary, it almost gives the impression of a comfortable maturity*

of something like a couple of hundred years. And yet there is nothing sham or old about it; it is not trumped up with any specious or fashionable devices of spurious antiquity; there is no pretending to be anything that it is not—no affectation whatever.[22] While on the other, for Julius Drewe, the founder of Home and Colonial Stores, the very 'castle' nature of the house was an essential part of the brief for Castle Drogo and Lutyens sighed *'. . . I do wish he did not want a castle, but a delicious lovely house with plenty of good large rooms in it.*[23]

Lutyens' approach was basically romantic and his houses were treated so as to appear to have grown through the ages. This attitude is found in the work of his forerunners. At St Albans Court, Nonington (1875) and Betteshanger Park, Deal (1856-82), George Devey gave the appearance of the patching and adaptation of decayed houses repaired at different dates. At Betteshanger this was achieved largely from the form and planning of the building, but at St Albans Court it is primarily from the use of materials; there an irregular stone base of some notional antiquity implied a ruined house whose walls had been reused as the lower courses of later brickwork. Philip Webb reduced the bulk of Standen (1891) by giving it the appearance of a house added to over a period of two hundred years and the main block of the building is treated as a seventeenth-century farmhouse standing in front of a background of buildings of indeterminate date.

This tendency to create a fictitious history for his buildings is seen in the interiors of Lutyens' early houses. The introduction of an eighteenth-century style bolection moulded chimney-piece into a vernacular house created the illusion of a minor modernisation at a date later than the original construction. The Corinthian pilasters in the hall at Marshcourt stand on timber pedestals rusticated in the form of brickwork; their 'artisan mannerist' appearance puts the apparent date of the construction of the body of the house beyond the seventeenth century and the mixture of styles in the decoration of rooms throughout Marshcourt implies a process of continuous modernisation and change. Externally the same occurs. Because of the contrast of style the Tuscan loggia at Tigbourne Court appears as a later insertion into a seventeenth-century vernacular house; and because of the contrast of construction the half-timbered sections of Overstrand Hall seem additions between masonry pavilions which appear as the fortified corner towers of an earlier house—a favourite Lutyens' motif found not only in vernacular houses but also in the corner pavilions of the north front of Great Maytham. The mixture of materials in the walls at Marshcourt makes the clunch appear randomly patched with tile and flint; the galletting of the joints and the banding of the Bargate stone with red tiles gives Tigbourne a timeless quality because of its impression of almost Roman solidity; at Grey Walls, where slips of grey pantile decorate the window lintels, a sense of continuity is achieved by the use of a local material in an unusual way. Occasionally the idea is expanded from an incident to the whole, so that houses appear as a group of buildings of different dates.

For the 'Shakespeare's England' exhibition at Earls Court in 1912, Lutyens reconstructed Exeter's Guildhall next to a seventeenth-century wing of St John's College, Oxford, but in a preliminary sketch for Castle Drogo (1910) the same college had appeared attached to a Norman Tower balanced by a version of his own stable block at Orchards to give the appearance of construction through eight centuries. The sequential experience of a house sited on the far side of a courtyard was supported by an historical fantasy at St Peter's House, Ipswich, where a 'William and Mary' house, similar to Folly Farm, was approached past a series of 'mediaeval' tithe barns. In his project (1901) for speculative housing at Rossal Beach in Lancashire, small individual houses are grouped in the plan of a Palladian mansion, but in elevation they appear to have been constructed at various dates in different materials and styles; the asymmetry of some houses implies a symmetry which has been lost with the overlay of later buildings.

The close observation and obvious enjoyment of the way historic buildings had been altered through the ages influenced Lutyens in the design of his completely new house at Ednaston. From the north it is clear that a vernacular house was encased at a later date with 'Wrennaissance' elevations on the three sides that a visitor might see, but the rear of the house towards the service yard was left unmodernised, retaining its gables. The same idea of development continues further on the flank walls of the south elevation, where stone doorcases overlap the classical pilasters, resulting in an effect of encrustation over a period of time. These devices were used mainly for romantic purposes but also solved architectural problems. The articulation of the service wing as a later extension at Little Thakeham and at The Salutation obviated solving the problem of including the large amount of kitchen accommodation within the symmetrical mass of the main building, and I have mentioned how the eighteenth-century handling of the screen wall across the face of Grey Walls disengaged it from the rest of the vernacular house and allowed the diagonal drive to terminate.

When Lutyens was concerned with an extension he often differentiated his addition from the existing building to preserve the clarity of the original intentions. This is apparent at Lambay, where the new kitchen court was disengaged from the original castle through plan and form. The same is true of Crooksbury and Folly Farm where Lutyens extended his own designs, but in these cases the separation was reinforced by the use of an invented history. In the former the vernacular house was extended with a suave William and Mary wing and in the latter the reverse occurred and the addition of a new dining room was treated as a vernacular 'cowshed'[24] to preserve the integrity of the early eighteenth-century style pavilion. In both cases the classical idiom gives predominance to one part over the other. At Crooksbury the extension was emphasised, while at Folly Farm the later wing was suppressed.

The previous examples are concerned with growth and

enlargement but Lutyens also used his attitude to historical styles to imply reduction and decay. The fragmentary quality of Castle Drogo makes the reduced house comprehensible by its implication of a once symmetrical building arranged about a U-shape court. The incompletion of the 'Gibbsian' remodelling of the 'Jacobean' Hall at Little Thakeham is implied by the fragmentation of the screen wall itself, giving the staircase a temporary quality which makes ambiguous whether the main axis of the house is also the central axis of the hall; which can then be considered symmetrically arranged about the oriel rather than around the fireplace located off axis as discussed earlier. At Nashdom the unused entrance court and the inaccessible front door stranded several feet above the level of the court imply the removal of a flight of steps, which gives the house a romantic history bringing to mind the steps lost at Houghton Hall in a gambling debt or the gates at Ham House never opened since the flight of James II. Even more romantic is Homewood, an elm weatherboarded cottage whose mass is cut back to reveal the white-rendered Ionic façade of a classical villa

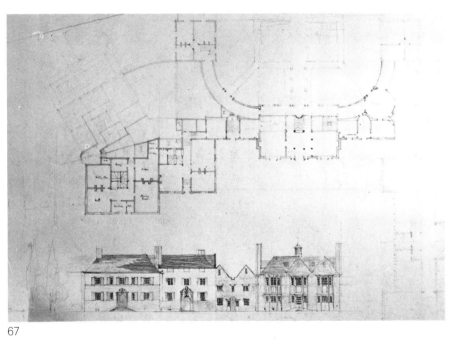

67

68

69   70

within. The reverse of Ednaston, the idea is concerned with the villa's decay and nature's growth, the metaphorical overgrowth itself being swamped by *Vitis Cognetiae* in the original early photographs.

Homewood is a fitting example with which to conclude this essay. It embodies most of the ideas discussed: the careful response to the requirements of the client, his mother-in-law; the west approach readjusted to a south orientation; the experience of the house enlarged by a complex circulation pattern and by the inclusion of the geometrically terraced site within the orbit of the building; the corners of the house marked by residual towers; and the house and terraces guarded by fictive sentry boxes cut in the supporting yew hedges. As well as the 'archaeological' decay described, paradox underlies the whole and unifies Homewood as much as geometry unifies Heathcote. Although hinted at by the relationship of the lodge to the drive, the axial approach to the house is only revealed halfway down the main drive which is suddenly relegated to the function of a service route. A large brightly lit stair is discovered

within the centre of a rather low, dark villa, a classical villa surprisingly within a cottage and a vernacular cottage within formal terraces.

Finally, however, it must be said that in many ways the experience of Lutyens' houses can be claustrophobic. They are so dependent on fantasies of a make-believe world that they lack that spontaneity of the direct solution so admired by Lutyens in the work of Philip Webb and from whom so much of Homewood, in particular, was derived. While it might be appropriate for the home of a dowager countess to be concerned with romantic decay, the intended enlargement eventually seems to inflate the house to an overblown scale and the hermetic world of idiosyncratic jokes becomes possibly precious and even overworked in its monotony. Without achieving the radical *conceptual* breakthrough of his American and European counterparts, however, Lutyens' houses often attain brilliance in their architectural solutions and stand, in any case, head and shoulders above the work of his English contemporaries.

71 Ednaston 1913 — the 'unmodernised' north front (CL 1923)
72 Homewood 1901 — romantic overgrowth (CL c.1905)

71

72

Notes

Owners and occupiers of houses have generously allowed the author access when he requested it and he feels that he must protect them from importunity by stating that only four Lutyens' houses are at present open to the public: Great Maytham, Kent, and Great Dixter, Sussex, are open occasionally, and Castle Drogo, Devon, and Lindisfarne Castle, Northumberland, are both properties of the National Trust.
In addition, the author would like to thank Peter Jenkins for reading the manuscript of this essay and making several useful suggestions about the defensive character of Lutyens' plans.

1 The plans of the houses and gardens were redrawn on the basis of those published in *Houses and Gardens by E.L. Lutyens* by Sir Lawrence Weaver, London 1913 and *The Architecture of Sir Edwin Lutyens* by A.S.G. Butler, London 1950. Additional information was derived from articles on individual houses published in *Country Life,* as well as first-hand measurements. The internal arrangement of the outbuildings is generally assumed and included to give an architectural cohesion to the whole. In some cases later extensions have been omitted.
2 Inskip, P., 'The Compromise of Castle Drogo', *Architectural Review,* April 1979.
3 Hussey, C., *The Life of Sir Edwin Lutyens,* London 1950.
4 Jekyll, Gertrude, *Old West Surrey: Some Notes and Memories,* London 1904.
5 Hussey, *op.cit.*
6 Brandon Jones, J., 'Reminiscences of Sir Edwin Lutyens' *Architectural Association Journal,* March 1959.
7 Correspondence of Lady Emily Lutyens to Sir Edwin Lutyens, April 29, 1911.
8 Correspondence of Sir Edwin Lutyens to Lady Emily Lutyens, August 27, 1909.
9 *Idem.,* August 4, 1909.
10 *Idem.,* June 8, 1912.
11 *Idem.,* April 18, 1913.
12 *Idem.,* Whit Monday 1910.
13 Inskip, P., *op.cit.*
14 Lutyens believed so strongly in the quasi-internal nature of his gardens that in the 1930s he jokingly

designed Sir Saxton Noble a complete house, larger than the Viceroy's house, to be made almost entirely of yew hedges and watercourses, with a ruined staircase forming a rockery. Only a tiny fragment was to be actually inhabitable but that 'just a bit pomposo'.
15 Correspondence of Sir Edwin Lutyens to Lady Emily Lutyens, March 19, 1910.
16 A late drawing by Lutyens in the RIBA Drawings Collection illustrates a discarded proposal for a terraced garden to the east of Castle Drogo. It stresses the difficulty of placing any garden next to the building and was probably drawn only at the client's request.
17 Hussey, *op.cit.*
18 Lutyens' use of black was strongly influenced by William Nicholson, a close friend and collaborator on the decoration of Folly Farm. Nicholson's series of woodcuts *An Almanac of Twelve Sports* was issued in 1898.
19 Hussey, *op.cit.*
20 The references to the colours used in the original decoration are largely from Sir Lawrence Weaver's *Houses and Gardens by E.L. Lutyens* (see above) and C. Hussey's *Life of Sir Edwin Lutyens* (see above) as well as first-hand examination of the houses.
21 Lutyens, R., *Sir Edwin Lutyens: an Appreciation in Perspective,* London 1942.
22 Gertrude Jekyll, *Home and Garden,* London 1900.
23 Correspondence of Sir Edwin Lutyens to Lady Emily Lutyens, August 3, 1910.
24 Lutyens, R., *op.cit.*

Orchards
1897-99
Munstead, Surrey

An L-shaped house is extended by a gateway, a studio and a cloister to form a square entrance court. The buttressed stable block, an extension of one side of this courtyard, implies an introductory courtyard outside the house and leads the visitor to the double-height entrance gateway, with the simple porch across the enclosed courtyard. The containment of the formal gardens to the north-east of the house by a 'rampart' walk emphasises the drama of discovering the distant views of the Hogs Back.

The materials are local Bargate stone, brick chimney-stacks and red roof tiles. The windows are leaded lights in metal casements set in oak frames. Red tiles set as voussoirs accentuate archways in the cloister and garden walls.

1 Plan
2 View over the Dutch Garden looking north towards the Hogs Back
3 Studio to the south of the entrance arch
4 The dining room loggia looking south from the Dutch Garden (CL 1901)

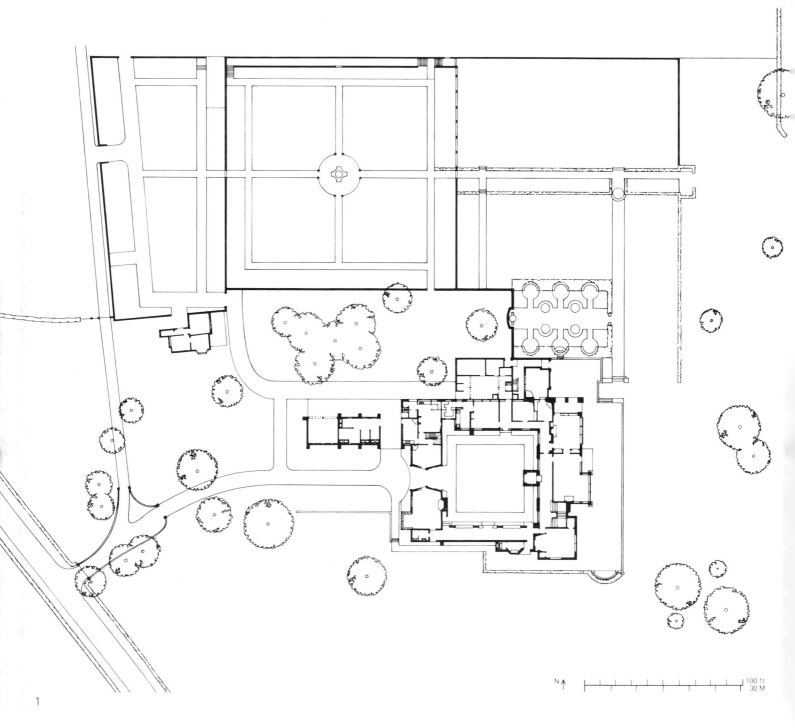

1

N↑ |—|—|—|—|—|—| 100 ft
                     30 M

2

3

4

Tigbourne Court
1899
Witley, Surrey

A symmetrical entrance court facing west leads to an L-shaped plan facing south and east. A billiard room was added in the north-west corner at a later date. From the house a pergola of irregularly spaced and alternating circular and square, brick columns leads into the garden. The sequence of entry court — vestibule — hall is remarkable for the studied symmetry of each asymmetrically entered space. The drawing room has both bi-axial symmetry and a major longitudinal axis terminating in a fireplace inglenook beneath an unlit dome.

Walls are of Bargate stone, galletted joints with courses of diagonally laid roof tiles set in the entrance façade. Red tiles are set as voussoirs in gateways and red bricks used in the entrance loggia, chimney-stacks and as window surrounds.

1 Plan
2 View of entrance court from the road
3 West, south, east and north elevations drawn by Lutyens 1899 (BAL/RIBA)

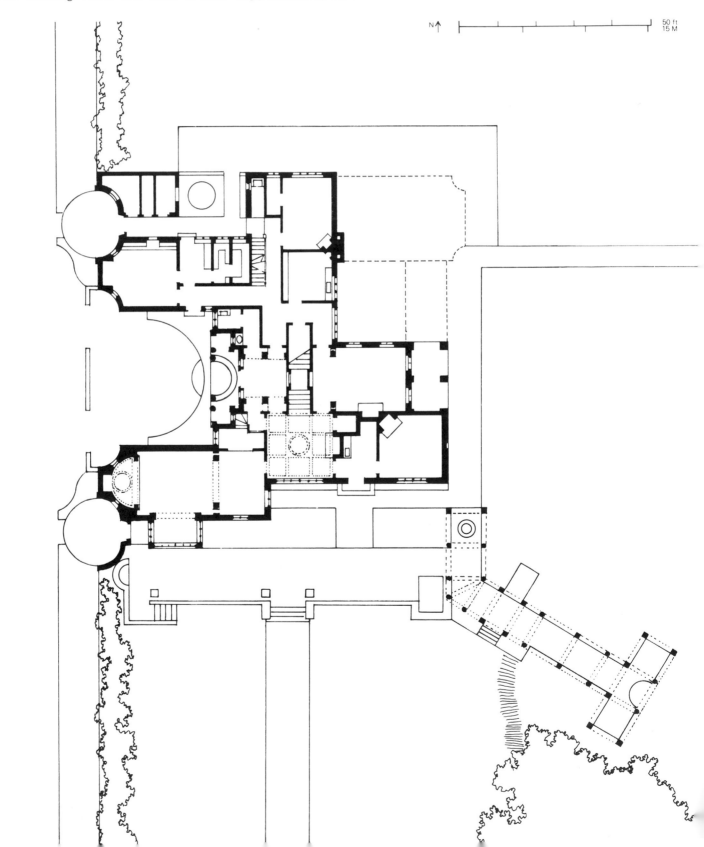

N↑

50 ft
15 M

1

2

3

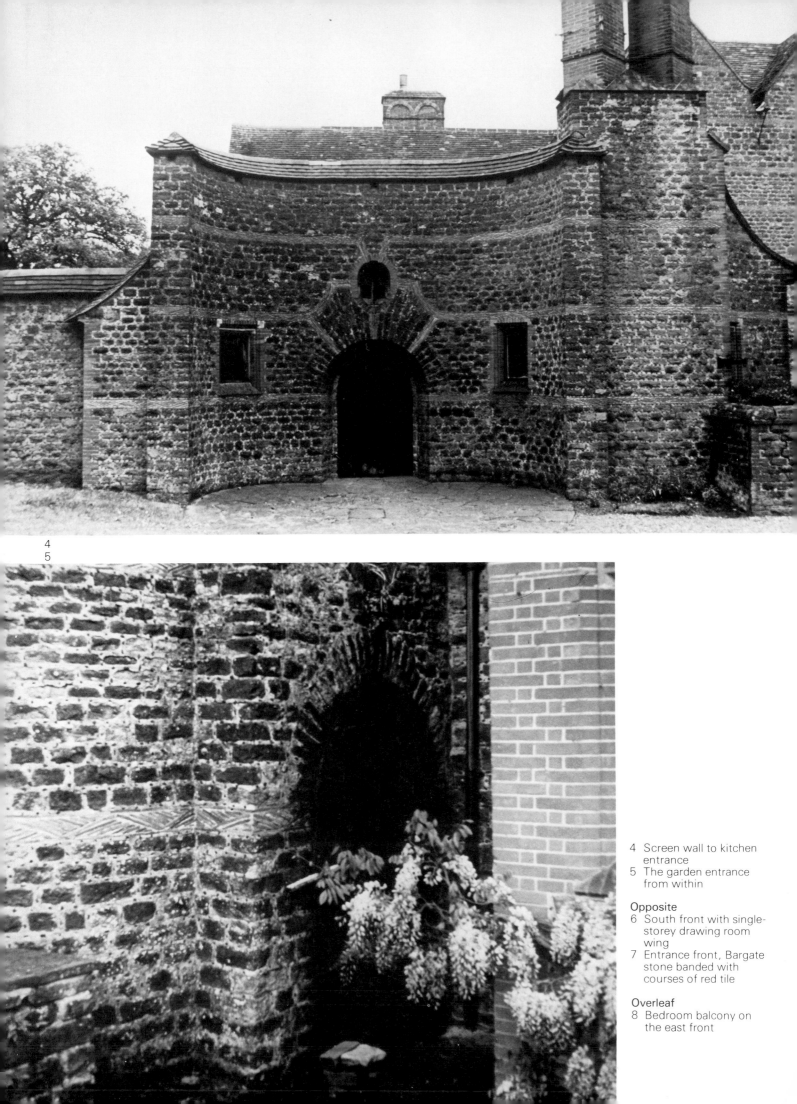

4
5

4 Screen wall to kitchen
  entrance
5 The garden entrance
  from within

Opposite
6 South front with single-
  storey drawing room
  wing
7 Entrance front, Bargate
  stone banded with
  courses of red tile

Overleaf
8 Bedroom balcony on
  the east front

Previous page
1   The axial approach to
    Homewood discovered
    halfway down the drive
2   The dining room
    windows in an Ionic
    façade revealed in the
    east elevation

Opposite
3   West entrance
    forecourt. The elm
    weather boarding was
    originally intended to
    be left a natural, silver
    grey, but has now been
    stained black
4   The omitted tympanum
    of the porch, leading to
    the front door on the
    right-hand wall
5   View from porch

6   Plan

Homewood
1901
Knebworth, Hertfordshire

An immensely sophisticated approach conceals
the axial drive to the house, although the lodge
indicates the arrangement. The small elm-
weatherboarded cottage gradually reveals itself as
a white-painted stuccoed classical villa. A
diagonal movement through the house to the
south is established at the porch where a classical
entrance door is set deeply within and to one side
of the porch. Here the detailing is richly
ambiguous: the rusticated reveals appear as
Tuscan pilasters, the tympanum of the pediment
is omitted to light the interior of the porch and the
expressed voussoirs of the flat arch, which should
form the base of the pediment, support nothing
but their own weight.

The staircase, similar to that of Tigbourne, rises
between parallel walls in the centre of the house to
a large top-lit landing and contains internal
windows through which the entrance vestibule
borrows light. Terracing of the gently sloping site
enlarges the house by implying that sections of
the garden are square enclosures allied to the
house.

39

Grey Walls
1900
Gullane, Scotland

The approach from the south-west on the diagonal is separated and planned so as not to compromise the southerly orientation of a basically H-shaped house. A curved screen wall between two pylon-like chimney-stacks allows this diagonal drive to terminate at one corner of the building from which pavilions and garden walls in the same cream-coursed rubble walls extend the symmetrical composition of this screen to include the whole entry court. Their plan makes these walls appear a series of wings, like theatrical flats, stepping out in support of the house to locate the entrance lodges, garage

buildings and gardener's cottage. The contrast of planted and open courts exaggerates their scale and the combination of diagonal and orthogonal routes with curved garden walls gives the visitor a sense of continuous discovery as unexpected relationships are revealed.

Within the rubble walls, curved pieces of grey pantile galletted with dots of red tile decorate the window lintels. These same Dutch pantiles are used for the roof, as a coping to the garden wall and atop the chimney-stacks.

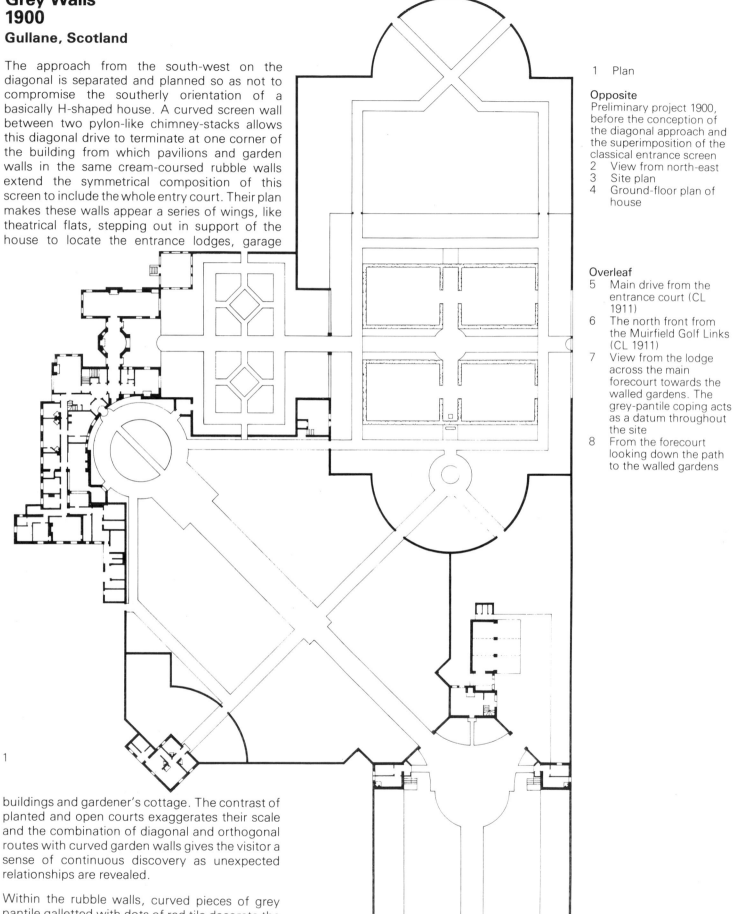

1

1   Plan

Opposite
Preliminary project 1900, before the conception of the diagonal approach and the superimposition of the classical entrance screen
2   View from north-east
3   Site plan
4   Ground-floor plan of house

Overleaf
5   Main drive from the entrance court (CL 1911)
6   The north front from the Muirfield Golf Links (CL 1911)
7   View from the lodge across the main forecourt towards the walled gardens. The grey-pantile coping acts as a datum throughout the site
8   From the forecourt looking down the path to the walled gardens

N   50 ft
15 M

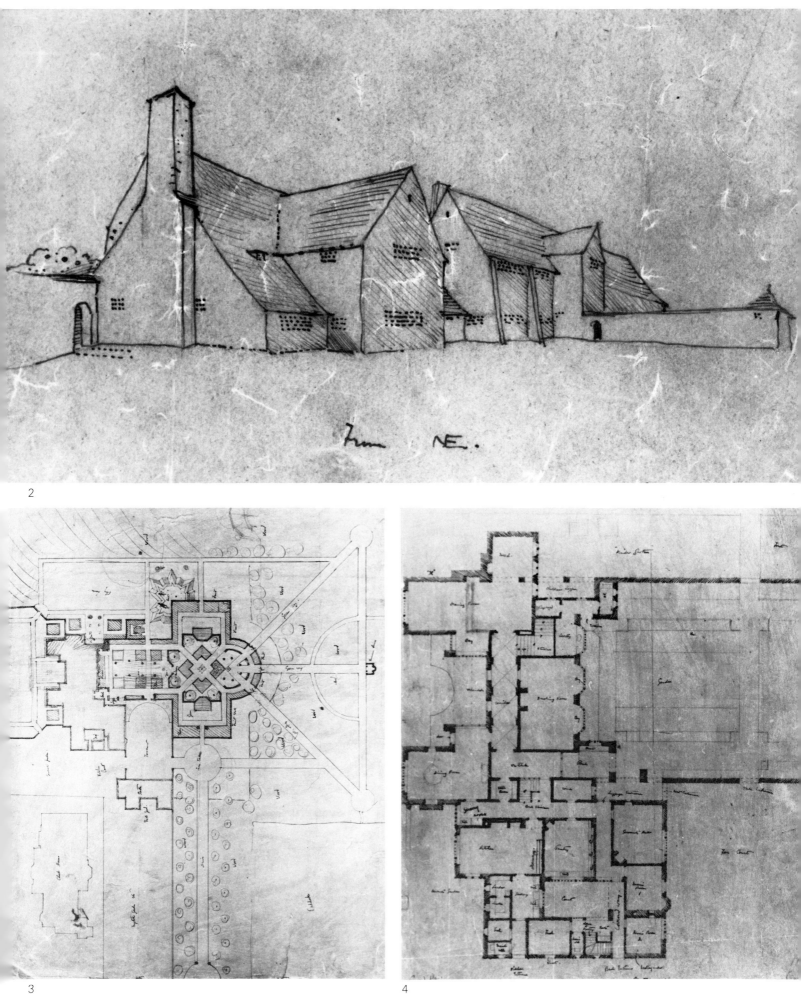

2

3

4

5

6

7

8

Rush Court
c. 1902
Berkshire

This proposed, stone country house project turns away from the vernacular. The preliminary designs for a large country house continue the 'Wrennaissance' theme used by Lutyens in his asymmetrical addition to Crooksbury of 1898. It can be dated to c.1901-02: the leaded light, transomed windows and classical detailing of the doorways are all reminiscent of his alterations at Abbotswood.

Anticipating such houses as Heathcote and Nashdom, this is one of the earliest examples of a simple symmetrical exterior concealing a highly complex arrangement of internal volumes in both plan and section. The articulation of the service accomodation as a separate disengaged wing, so as not to disrupt the symmetry of the main body of the house, is similar to the treatment of both Little Thakeham and The Salutation

In many respects the design is overloaded and incoherent, but this is typical of Lutyens in his preliminary design drawings. As seen in the development of Nashdom, Castle Drogo and Ednaston, subsequent design stages usually involved considerable simplification of initial proposals.

1

2

1 North entrance front and south elevation to river (BAL/RIBA)
2 Section through house showing rich polychromy of materials in the decoration of the double-height hall (BAL/RIBA)
3 Ground-floor plan, — the service wing is extended to the south to an alcove to block out sight of neighbouring villas (BAL/RIBA)
4 First-floor plan - with double-height hall omitted (BAL/RIBA)

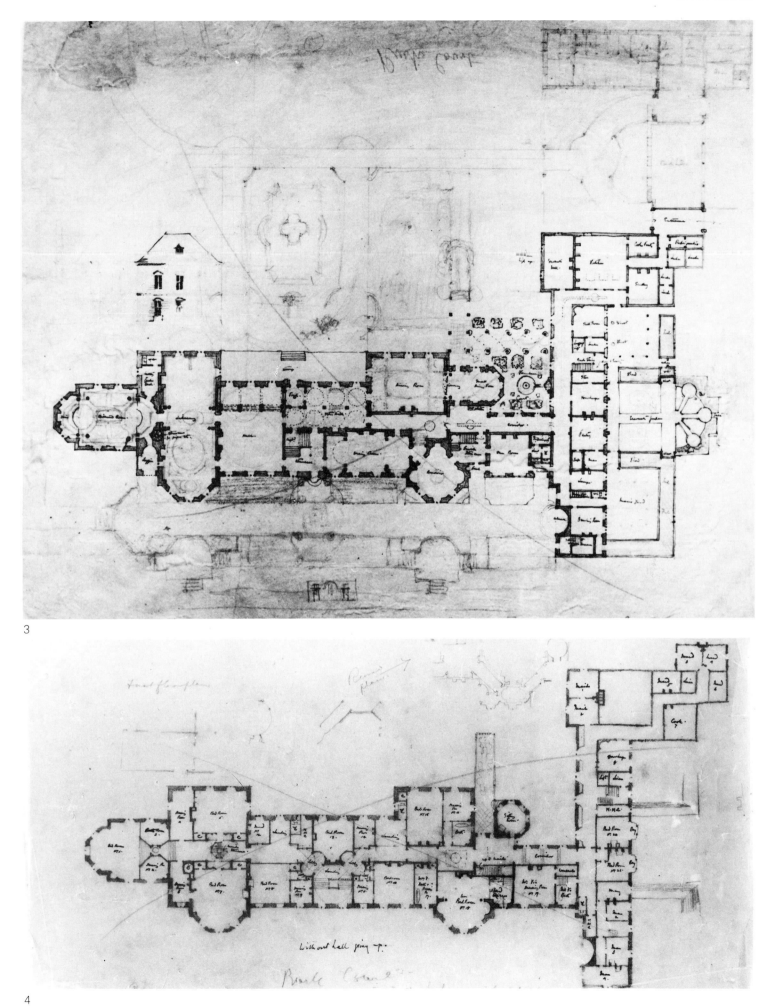

3

4

Deanery Garden
1901
Sonning, Berkshire

Three gateways penetrate an ancient brick wall enclosing the north end of an old orchard. Two wings extend from the house out to the wall to enclose an inner court with the central gateway leading down one side of this court through a low-vaulted passage to the front door. A screens passage interrupts a sequence of main rooms parallel to the road and continues out to the gardens which are again layered parallel to the road. The house and courtyard are arranged about an axis which in the double-height hall locates the large oriel window and fireplace, as well as the statue in the courtyard. However, the entrance passage which extends as the main axis of the garden is asymmetric to the mass of the house.

The building is constructed of red Berkshire brickwork under a tile roof with leaded lights set in oak window frames. Internally the brick walls are plastered, but the church ashlar, introduced in the groin vaulting of the entrance passage, continues

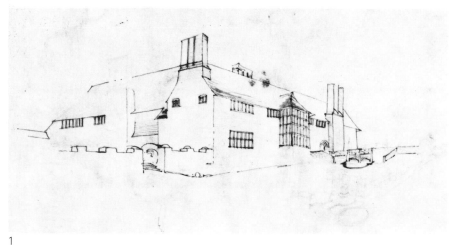

1

into the vestibule and stairway and is used as an infill between the oak wind bracing of the cross partitions in the hall. The construction of the stair is typical of Lutyens at this date; each dowel is clearly expressed, the space between the joists of the landing is left open to allow light to filter through to the vestibule below and the ends of the joists are beautifully finished with miniature coffers.

1 Preliminary sketch
2 Plan
3 Looking along the rill in the dry moat towards the bridge (CL 1913)
4 The axis from the courtyard to the garden crosses the entrance cloister (CL 1913)

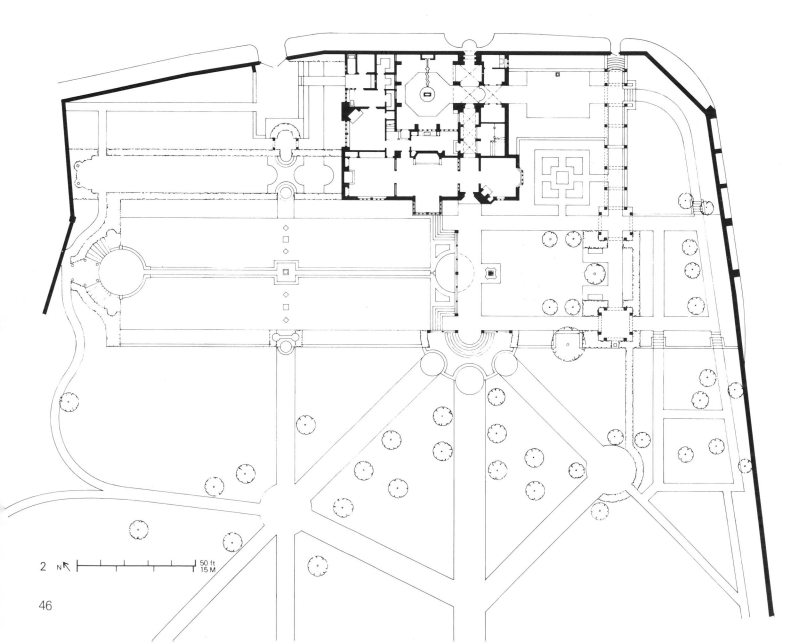

2 N |⊢—⊢—⊢—⊢—⊢—⊢⊣ 50 ft
15 M

Deanery Garden. The garden is one of Lutyens' and Miss Jekyll's finest collaborations. The iris channel (or 'rill') was an idea Miss Jekyll brought back from Moorish Spain

Deanery Garden. The garden elevation is one of Lutyens' most famous compositions, the great bay window balancing the massive chimney and arched entrance. It is the culmination of lessons learnt from Surrey and building Munstead Wood

3
4

Little Thakeham
1902
Thakeham, Sussex

The private drive approaching Little Thakeham is treated like a country lane from which the Tudor-style house is protected by a walled forecourt. Within, a quasi-Elizabethan great hall is entered via a screened passage treated as a fragment of a half-completed Baroque remodelling of the space. This screen also conceals the lower flights of the staircase, whose landing emerges as a gallery above the entrance passage and continues in stages to the door of the main bedroom.

Both in detailing and furnishing, the hall contrasts the grand and the humble. It is virtually independent of the exterior, its volume concealed behind a blank elevation through which only the oriel window declares the double-height space within.

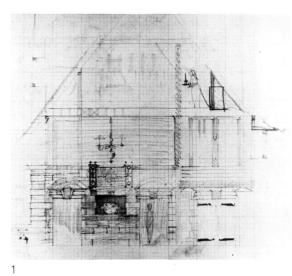

1

1   Study of section through the house showing hall and vestibule (BAL/RIBA 1902)
2   Plan
3   The garden door and hall oriel on the south front
4   The hall as built with the original simple furnishing (CL 1909)

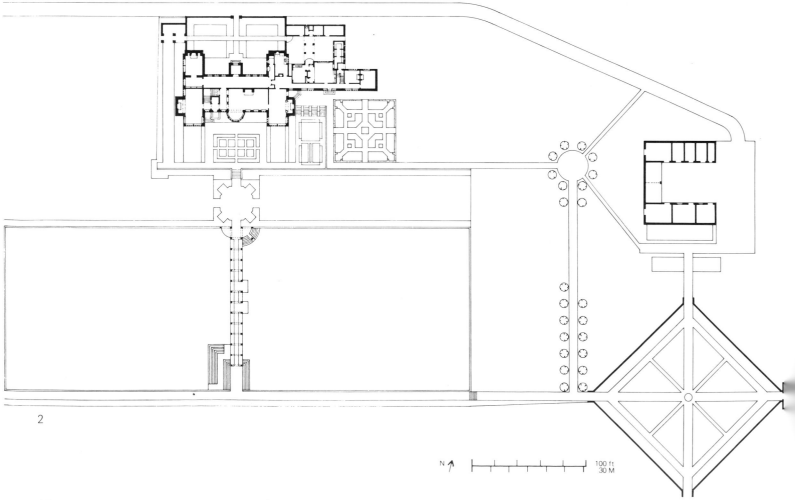

2

N ↑   100 ft / 30 M

3
4

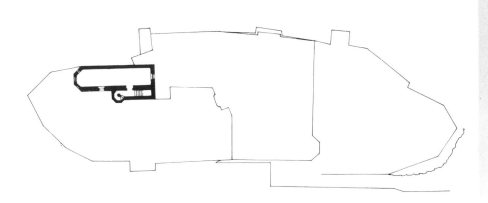

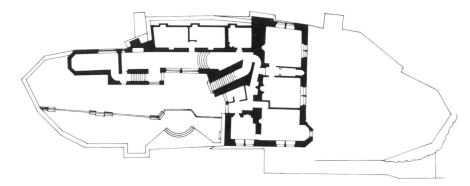

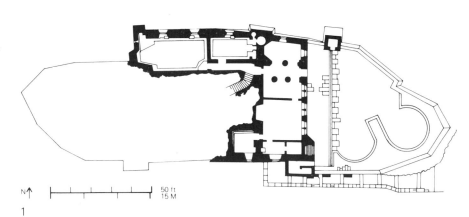

N↑ |‒‒‒‒‒‒‒| 50 ft / 15 M

1

2

Lindisfarne Castle
1903

Holy Island, Northumberland

Lutyens started to repair and renovate the ruined sixteenth-century fort in 1903, a year after its purchase by Edward Hudson, owner of *Country Life.* Externally he added a pantiled roof covering three new bedrooms beneath and remodelled elements such as windows and the tower at the west end. His primary achievement is the alternating sequence of internal and external spaces experienced by the visitor as he moves up between ramps, ramparts, staircases and rooms that appear to be hewn from rock.

3

1 Plans, tower, upper
  battery, lower battery
2 The castle isolated
  among highland cattle
  (CL 1913)
3 View from the east.
  The form of the lower
  battery greatly
  influenced the design
  of Castle Drogo
4 The entrance on the
  lower battery
5 In the gallery (CL 1913)

4

5

Marshcourt
1901-04
(extended 1924)
Kings Somborne, near Stockbridge, Hampshire

A moat and bridge complete the enclosure of a quadrangular entrance court to a basically E-shaped house. Bay windows and chimney-stacks break the south façade into vertical elements arranged irregularly in plan and contrast with the biaxial symmetry of the north front whose horizontality is supported by the first-floor corridor windows which almost appear as *fenêtre longeur*. The garden is contained with the house by a series of balaustraded terraces, pergolas and changes in level. Its closed forms contrast with open views across the valley of the River Trent. Within the building stylistic contrasts occur. Through the use of various period details rooms appear to have been decorated at later dates than the 'Tudor' style of the house. Outside, the random blocks of flint and tile seem insertions into the chalk ashlar of the walls which rise from a chequerboard band of chalk and flint. An early proposal for thatching the building was not executed.

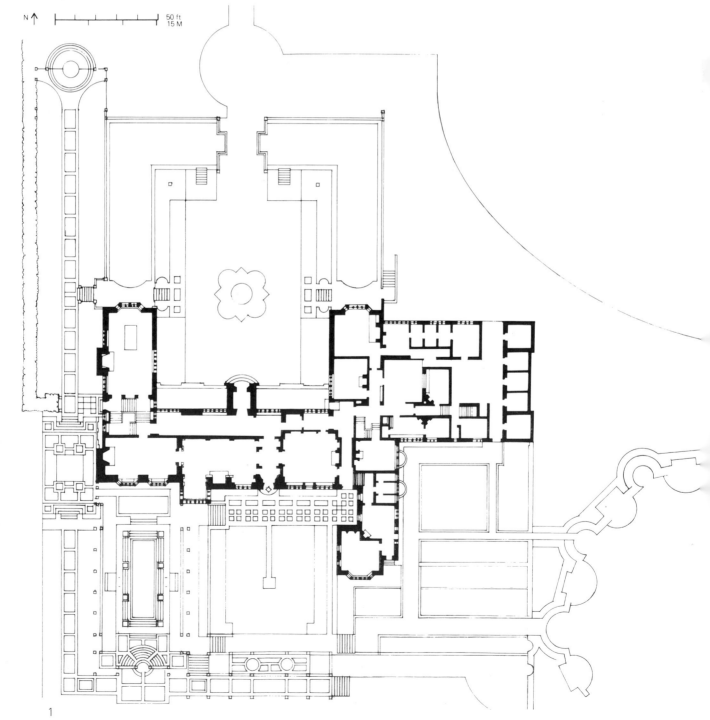

1

2

3

1 Plan
2 South and north
  elevations with early
  proposal for thatching
  (BAL/RIBA 1901)
3 View from south lawn
  over the Sunk Pool
  Garden (CL 1913)
  The publication of the
  exteriors was delayed
  seven years until the
  garden had matured

4

5

4 Artisan Mannerist details in the hall (CL 1906)
5 The dining room panelled in walnut (CL 1906)

Opposite
6 The hall bay window   Photograph: Tim Bell
7 Clunch wall inset with red tiles and grey flints

Overleaf
8 The Sunk Pool Garden
9 Loggia on south terrace

Papillon Hall
1903
(now demolished)
Market Harborough, Leicestershire

1 View from entrance loggia into the Basin Court (CL 1912)
2 Plan

Overleaf
3 East side (CL 1912)
4 The classical entrance loggia embedded in the vernacular house leads to the Basin Court concealed by a screen wall to the left (CL 1912)
5 The Basin Court and the front door (CL 1912)

A rectilinear entrance court leads, via a porch embedded in one of the wings of the house, through an external court surrounded by a Tuscan columed cloister to the entrance vestibule on the west side of the building. The basically H-shaped plan is symmetrically disposed for views to south and east. At the centre of the H, circulation is peripheral with all principal rooms having two doors leaving the major axis to originate from a wall and continue out into the garden. The entrance sequence was differentiated from the vernacular house by classical detailing and the interior was decorated in a variety of eclectic styles.

1

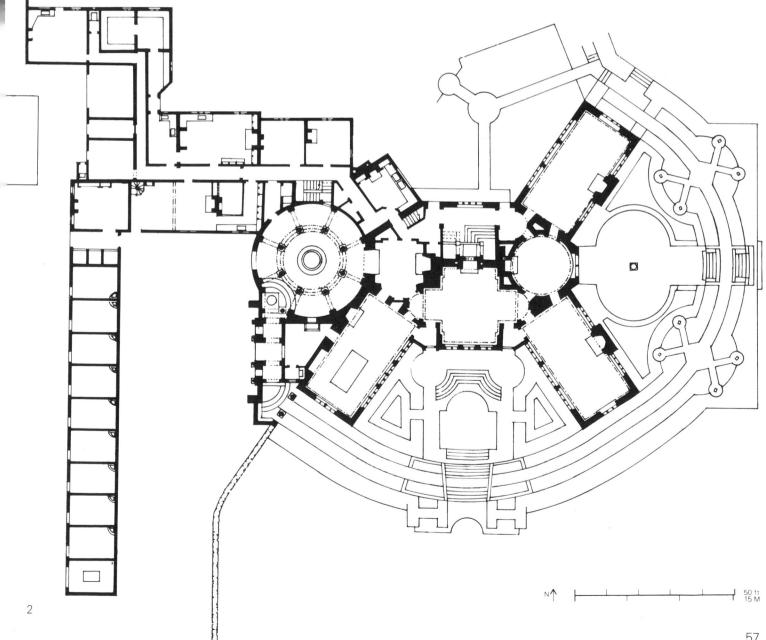

2

N↑　　　　　　　　　　　50 ft
　　　　　　　　　　　　15 M

Harriman House
1903

On the Hudson River, New York, USA

'This morning called on Mr Harriman the multi-millionaire. I am to make sketches for a house— money no object! Whether I get the job or no is another matter—all America is after the job.' Letter from Lutyens to Lady Emily Lutyens, August 10, 1903.

A scheme for a courtyard house approached from the east exploiting a sloping site. Flights of steps within the court lead up to the entrance and double-height great room at the level of the west terrace. Across this room full-width steps rise to the grand staircase at the north end and descend

to the salon in the centre of a linear progression of reception rooms along the south terrace. The reorientation and general arrangement recalls both Tigbourne and Homewood, while the tall, urban, Palazzo-like elevation concealing the terracing of the site anticipates Nashdom.

Given that the drawings represent only preliminary proposals, Spanish and Italian influences can be clearly discerned as well as the influence of Jones and Chambers. However, the overlapping of elements on the south elevation is completely typical of Lutyens' work.

1 Site plan, an east approach (right) readjusted to a south orientation

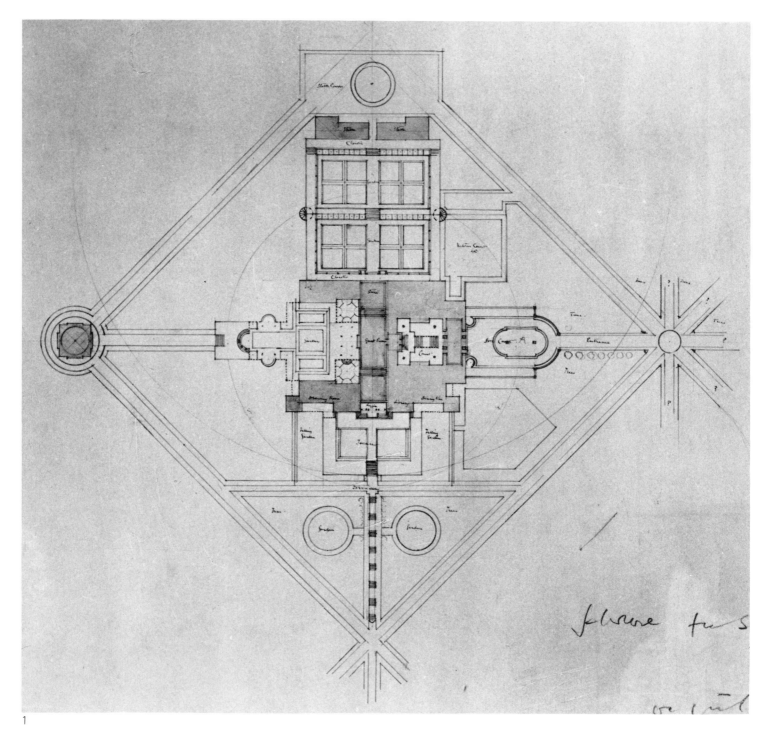

1

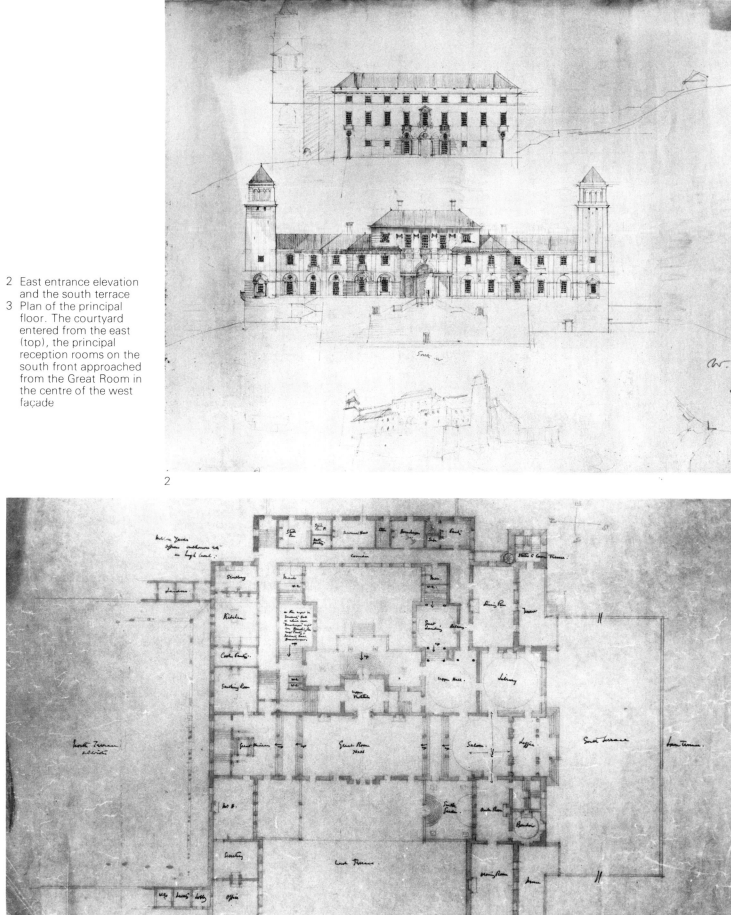

2 East entrance elevation and the south terrace
3 Plan of the principal floor. The courtyard entered from the east (top), the principal reception rooms on the south front approached from the Great Room in the centre of the west façade

2

3

Opposite
1 The south terrace in its heyday outside the winter garden (CL 1912)

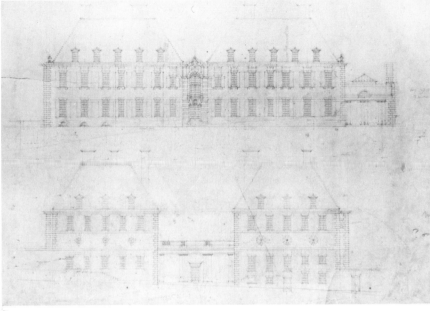

2

2 Preliminary study for south and north elevations in a rather more ornate French style than the final neo-Georgian façade
3 Plan

Nashdom
1905-09
Taplow, Buckinghamshire

Intended as a large but inexpensive house for entertaining, Nashdom cost £15,000 — over double the original target of £6,000 set by Prince Alexis Dolgorouki. The almost urban, neo-Georgian elevations, considerably simplified in the design stages, are surprisingly pure and bare but the whitewashed brickwork is decorated with apple-green shutters on the south elevation and enlivened above the parapet line by a red-tiled roof from which large, red-brick chimney-stacks, finished with stone cornices, rise confidently.

From the road, the house conceals the dramatic terracing of the steeply sloping site, but the change from a five-storey entrance façade to a three-storey south elevation is not well resolved at the west end.

Although appearing as one house in plan the building is divided by three 'external' spaces: the entrance loggia, the apsidal court and the double-height, top-lit winter garden. However, the court is unused and a peripheral entrance route links the suite of reception rooms on the south front round the recessed court to the Tuscan loggia across the north front.

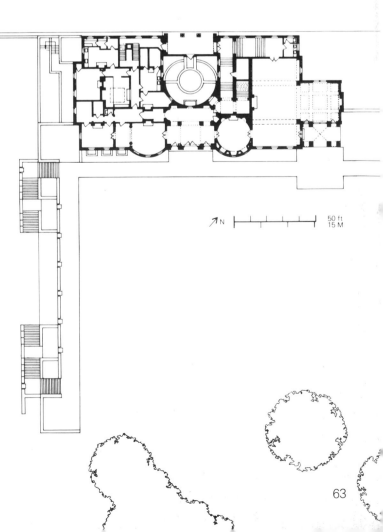

3

Overleaf
4 Winter Garden looking towards courtyard (CL 1912)

In colour
5 Winter Garden
6 North entrance front
7 South garden front. The original colours of white brickwork with green shutters enlivened by the red tiles and brick chimney stacks

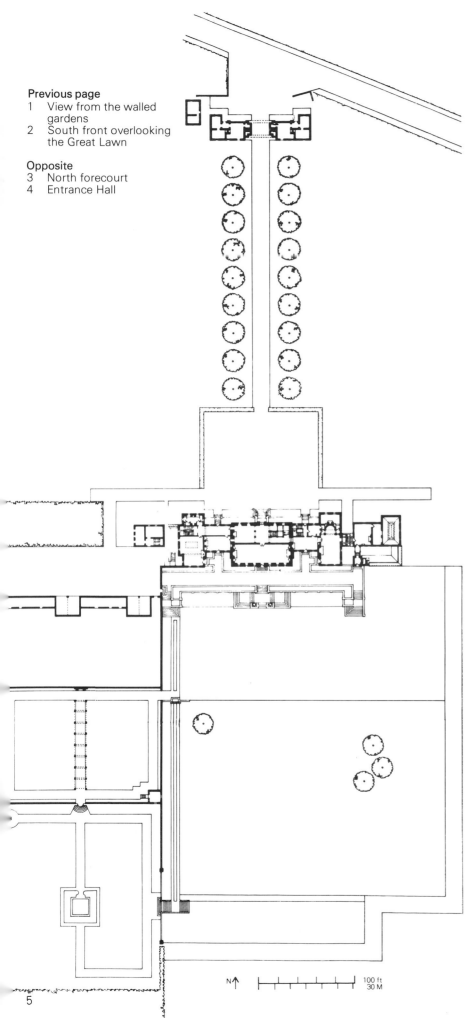

Great Maytham
1907-09
Rolvenden, Kent

The centre block incorporates a house constructed in 1721 but considerably altered in the nineteenth century. Lutyens added a third storey and a high, hip roof as well as encasing the building with 'Wrennaissance' elevations of blue-grey brick with red-brick dressings and stone doorcases. He extended the house to the east and west with wings terminated by pavilions which on the north front appear like towers, with the hip roofs rising to central chimney-stacks. White-painted timber sash windows set flush with the wall surface continue the planar quality of the wall, which today is relieved only by raised brick aprons although, originally, apple-green shutters decked the south elevation.

The axial approach passes through the entrance gateway under a large, hip roof surmounted by a clock tower, down a lime avenue and continues directly through the house out to the gently terraced lawn to the south marked only on the west by the edge of the existing walled gardens that Lutyens also remodelled.

5   Plan
6   View of the main house from the entrance lodges (CL 1912)

Overleaf
7   South front decked with apple-green shutters (now removed) (CL 1929)
8   Extension by Lutyens of the original walled gardens (CL 1929)

N↑   100 ft / 30 M

5

6

7
8

Heathcote
1906
King's Road, Ilkley, Yorkshire

Lutyens claimed a classical style was necessary to remove the house from the 'villadom' in which it was set in the suburbs of Ilkley and revelled in the 'high game of Palladio' while working on the designs for Heathcote. However, the style is far closer to the Edwardian Baroque of Norman Shaw and owes much to Vanbrugh and Giulio Romano in the handling of the wall surface and the coupled rusticated chimney-stacks. The red-pantile roof, recalling Philip Webb's work at Rounton and adding colour to the rather dour local stone, again removes it from the eighteenth century. Blocking the central axis within the house is certainly not found in Palladio and retains the circuitous patterns of circulation used to enlarge the experience of Lutyens' earlier houses such as Little Thakeham.

The terracing of the site and the treatment of house and garden as one pyramidal composition of horizontal planes contrasts strongly with the neighbouring picturesque suburban gardens. The cost of the building was £17,500.

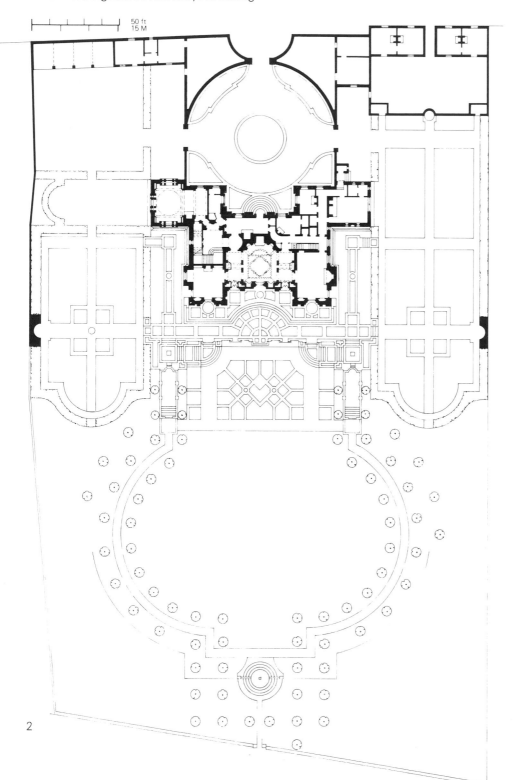

50 ft
15 M

2

Ednaston Manor
1912-13
Derbyshire

A surprisingly unprententious house for W. G.
Player, the cigarette manufacturer. Although
'Wrennaissance' in style, the low reception
rooms, small casements and the softness of the
red Bedfordshire brick relate the design to the
early vernacular houses. The gradual diagonal
movement through the building not only leads to
long vistas, but produces a sense of repose. Each
façade is strongly symmetrical and treated as a
series of layered elements; a string course
continues the forecourt walls across the entrance
façade, there is an encrustation of classical detail
on the flank walls of the south front and, from the
north, the house appears as a vernacular building
encased with classical elevations at a later date.

While the house and garden are distanced from
the surrounding park by brick walls and yew-
hedged enclosures, three radiating avenues
extend the influence of the entrance front beyond
the forecourt, but modesty prevails and the drive
is an oblique approach down one of the side
avenues.

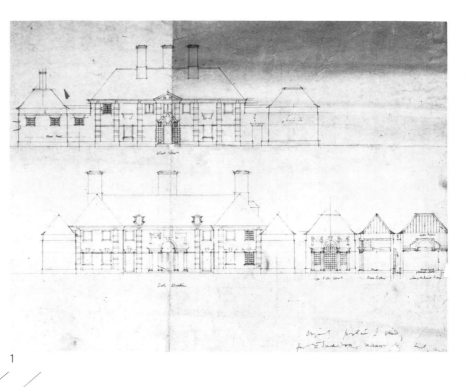

1

2

1 Preliminary scheme for larger house, west and south elevations (BAL/RIBA 1912)
2 Plan
3 Study for the south elevation, April 1913
4 West entrance court (CL 1923)

Overleaf
5 South terrace (CL 1923)
6 Staircase looking back to entrance vestibule (CL 1923)

In colour
7 View from the north-west
8 East garden

3

4

5
6

El Guadalperal
1915-28
near Toledo, Spain

Lutyens produced three projects for palaces in Spain. Each is organised around a courtyard and relies heavily on the local vernacular for its external appearance. The commission for El Guadalperal came in 1915. Although the design was complete in 1917 a further year elapsed before work began. The Duke of Penaranda insisted that the site works and outbuildings were started first, involving the laying of fourteen miles of new road to the hitherto inaccessible site, as well as the terracing of the gardens. A small temporary home was built on the site for the Duke but following his murder during the Spanish Civil War work on the then incomplete house was abandoned.

A scheme exists, in the RIBA Drawings Collection, for a smaller palace omitting the four wings which accommodated the Duke, the chapel court, the kitchen court, and the King when he visited. This scheme (not illustrated here) has different elevations. Simultaneously Lutyens reconstructed a large farmhouse at Ventosilla for the Duke's brother-in-law, which underlines the bucolic nature of El Guadalperal. Lutyens described the farmhouse as *'a Lambay in a sea of Spain'*.

Opposite, Ednaston Manor
9 North service yard
10 The south terrace. The capitals are designed to incorporate the initials of family members

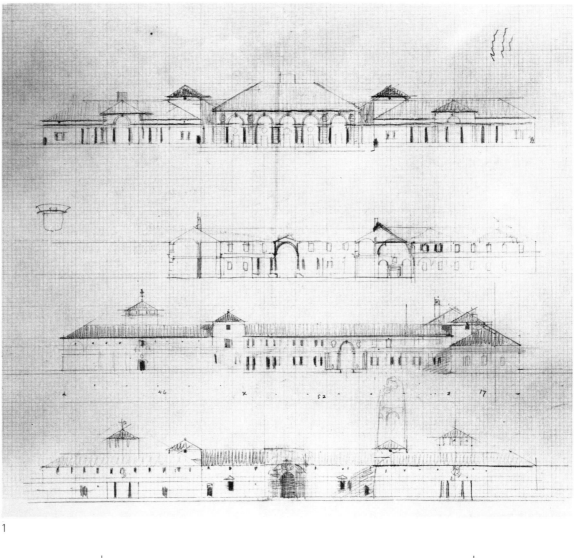

1

1 Preliminary study
c.1913 (BAL/RIBA)
a) south elevation, the duke's and king's wings either side of the main reception rooms
b) section through courtyard
c) west elevation
d) north elevation, the kitchen and chapel courts either side of the main entrance door
2 The developed form of the north elevation 1926 (redrawn)

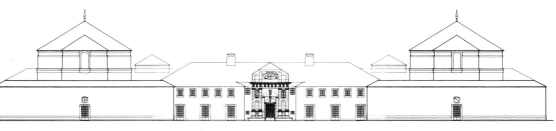

2

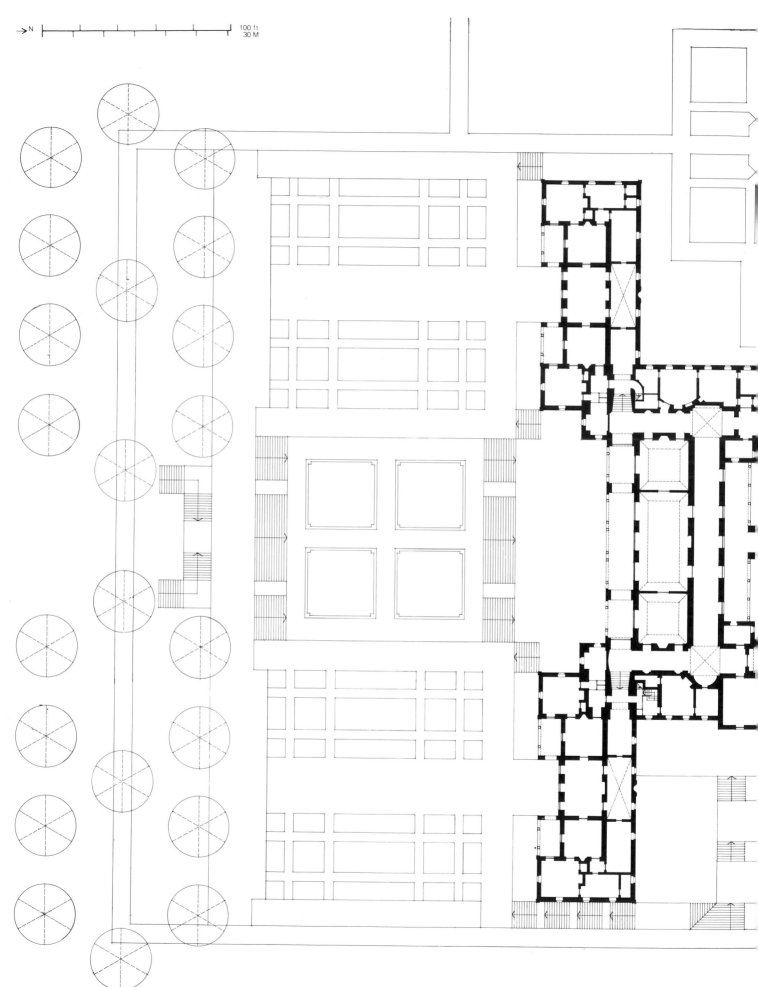

→N 100 ft
30 M

3 Plan

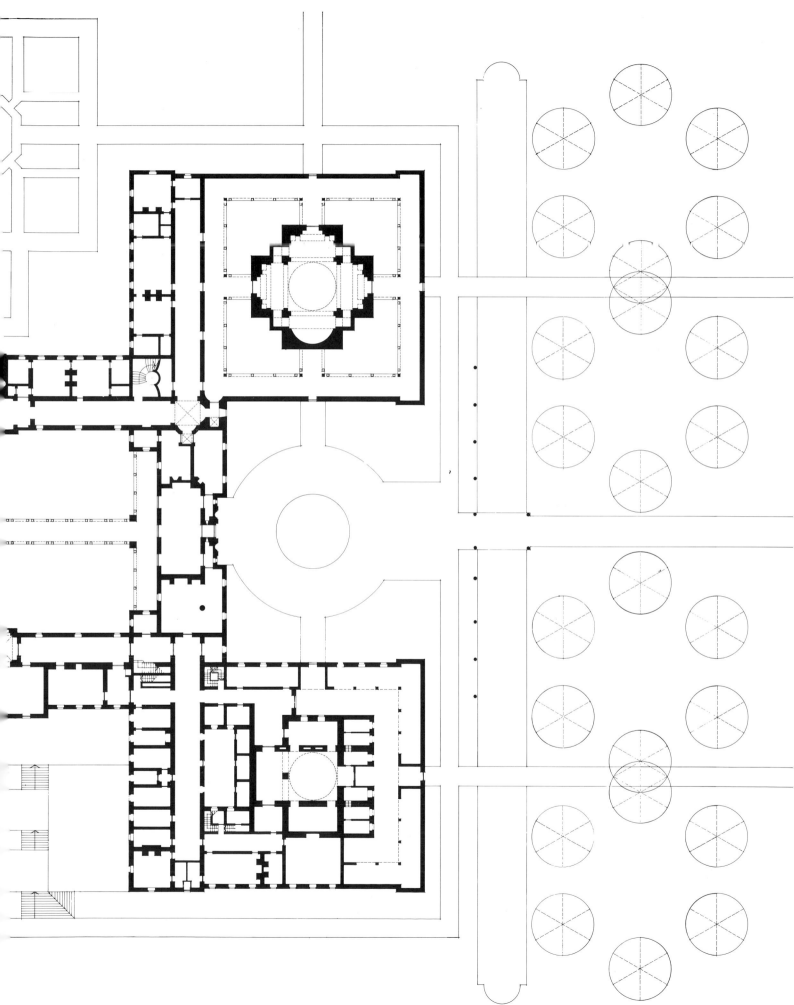

Lambay Castle
1905

County Dublin, Ireland

The rehabilitation and considerable enlargement of a derelict sixteenth-century fort on Lambay Island, off the coast of County Dublin, consciously preserved the primitive quality of the house and site. While Lutyens reconstructed the north-east front of the castle, the additional accommodation required for guests and service rooms was contained in a new kitchen court, disengaged diagonally from the main block and suppressed under a large roof. Further, the new building was cut into the sloping site and only connected to the castle on the ground floor by a passage below the east court. The two buildings are constructed of similar materials, rubble walls built of local porphyry with dressings of blue-grey limestone under grey-pantile roofs. The house and its gardens, farm buildings and plantations are united into one 'castle' by a circular rampart wall.

1 Plan
2 The North Tower 1905-08
3 Looking from house back along the approach from the harbour (CL 1929)

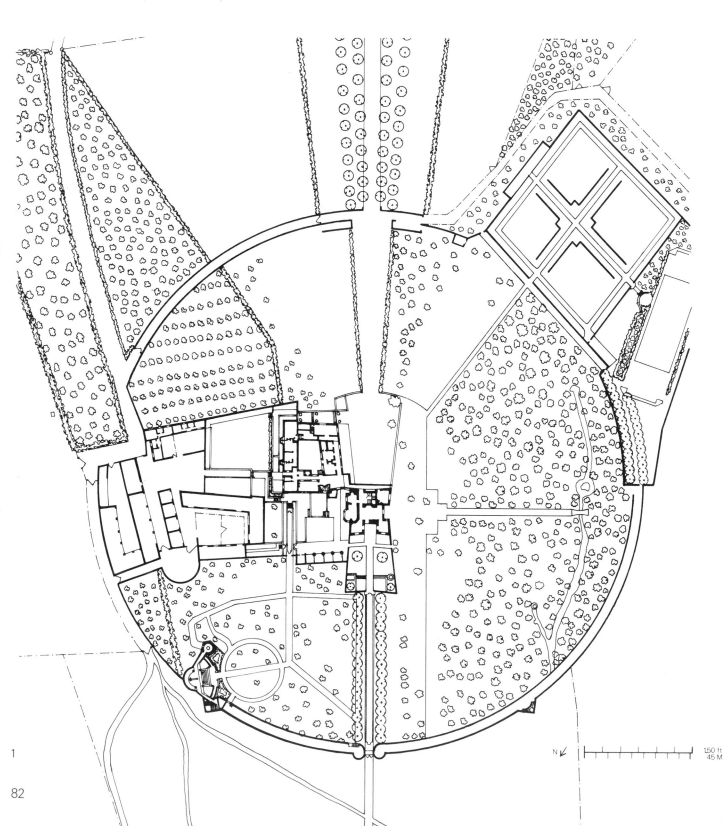

1

N

150 ft
45 M

2

3

4 View looking west over
the castle and jetty
towards the mainland
(CL 1929)
5 The original castle
extended with garden
walls and the kitchen
court (CL 1912)

Opposite,
6 Original building
adapted and furnished
by Lutyens showing
new arch and fireplace
in the sitting room. The
walls white-washed,
the floor painted duck-
egg blue (CL 1912)

4
5

Whalton Manor
1908-09
Whalton, Northumberland

A tripartite entrance arch and first-floor extension link four eighteenth-century village houses as one building. The east end had already been extended and was retained to provide sitting rooms. Lutyens reorganised the rest of the building, divided on the ground floor by the entrance arch, so that the rooms became the outer and inner halls connected up with a monumental staircase leading to an upper hall over the entrance and a circular dining room on the first floor. The whole is experienced as a continuous linear arrangement of reception rooms looking south towards the street; thus the view to the east is contained by the stone garden walls, while the view from the west looks out over the wall to the country beyond.

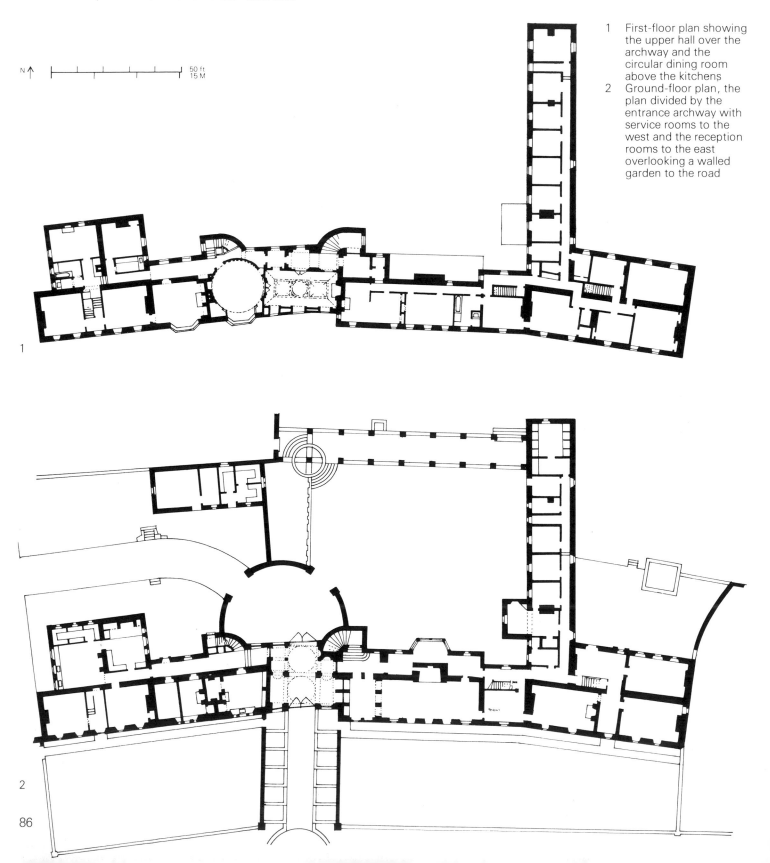

1 First-floor plan showing the upper hall over the archway and the circular dining room above the kitchens
2 Ground-floor plan, the plan divided by the entrance archway with service rooms to the west and the reception rooms to the east overlooking a walled garden to the road

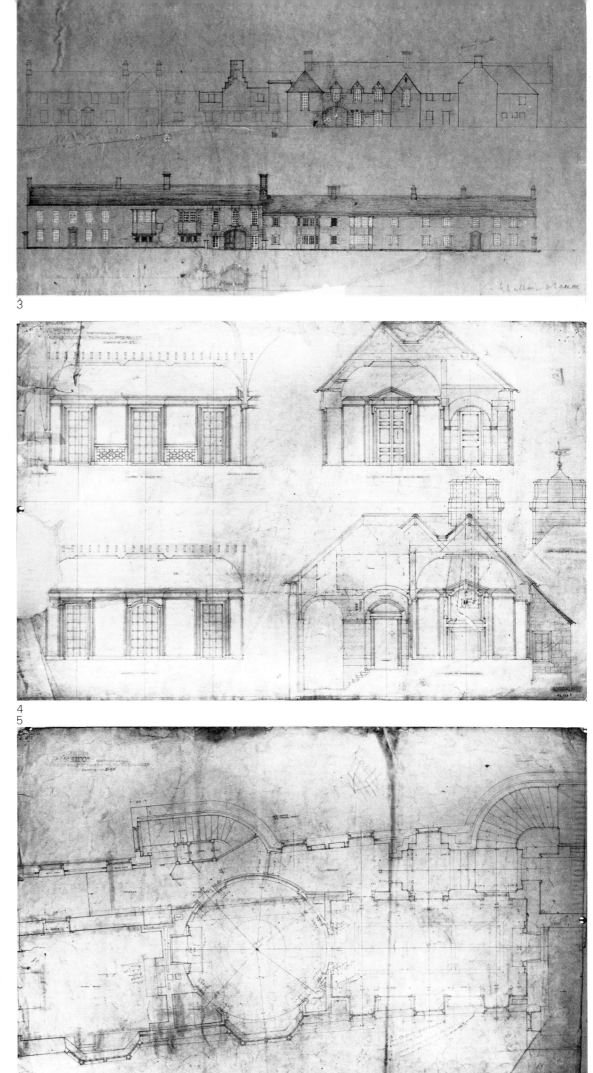

3 North and south
  elevations (BAL/RIBA
  1908)
4 Sectional elevations of
  the upper hall
  (BAL/RIBA 1909)
5 Plan of the addition at
  first-floor level showing
  the circular dining
  room, upper hall and
  head of staircase
  (BAL/RIBA 1909)

1

Castle Drogo
1910-30
Drewsteignton, Devonshire

Though construction started in 1911 on a vast new house arranged around three sides of a court, the scheme was halved the following year to a more manageable size by arbitrarily cutting the scheme on the centre-line of the original proposal. Further reductions followed the Great War and the foundations of the intended great hall were remodelled to form the chapel. Because of these changes, Lutyens proposed building an entrance gateway across the drive to re-establish the mass of the house from the north. Despite the construction of a full-scale mock-up in timber and canvas the idea was rejected by the client.

As work proceeded from the north tower to the south end, a *tour de force* of granite construction, the Tudor treatment of the house became simpler under the influence of Lutyens' work at New Delhi and Thiepval. The variation of the height of the principal bedrooms resulted in toof terraces at varying levels, treated almost as a *promenade architecturale*. Generally walls are battered, though some elements, for example the staircase window on the east face are vertical for emphasis. Granite construction is always apparent in the interior, even when progressively softened by overlays of oak, painted panelling and plaster.

3 Proposed north elevation- a Norman tower set between a version of Lutyens' own stable block at Orchards and seventeenth-century wing of St John's College, Oxford (BAL/RIBA 1910)
4 Proposed east elevation influenced by Germanic picturesque massing (BAL/RIBA 1910)

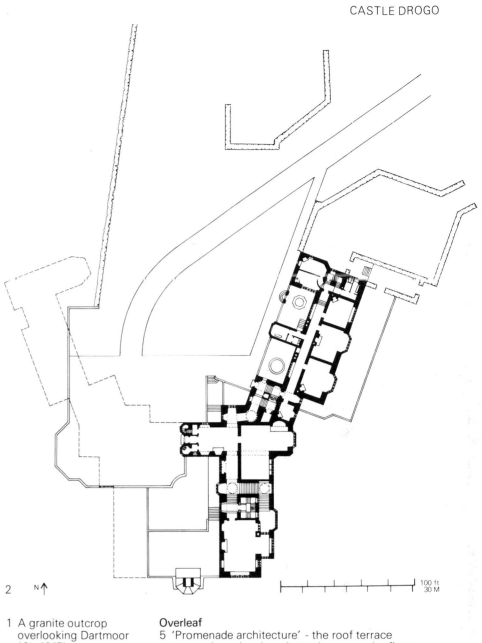

2   N↑

100 ft
30 M

1 A granite outcrop
overlooking Dartmoor
(CL 1945)

2 Plan - the dotted
outline indicates the
intended symmetrical
arrangement
abandoned in 1912

Overleaf
5 'Promenade architecture' - the roof terrace
responds to the changing volumes on the floor
below (CL 1945)
6 The library (CL 1945)
7 The lantern over the kitchen (CL 1945)
8 The pivotal staircase (CL 1945)
9 The kitchen with oak furniture designed by
Lutyens (CL 1945)

3

4

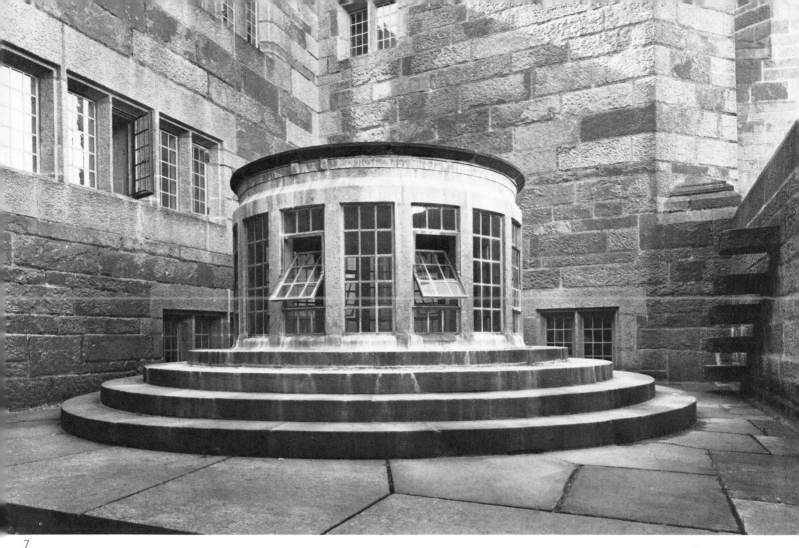

7

8

9

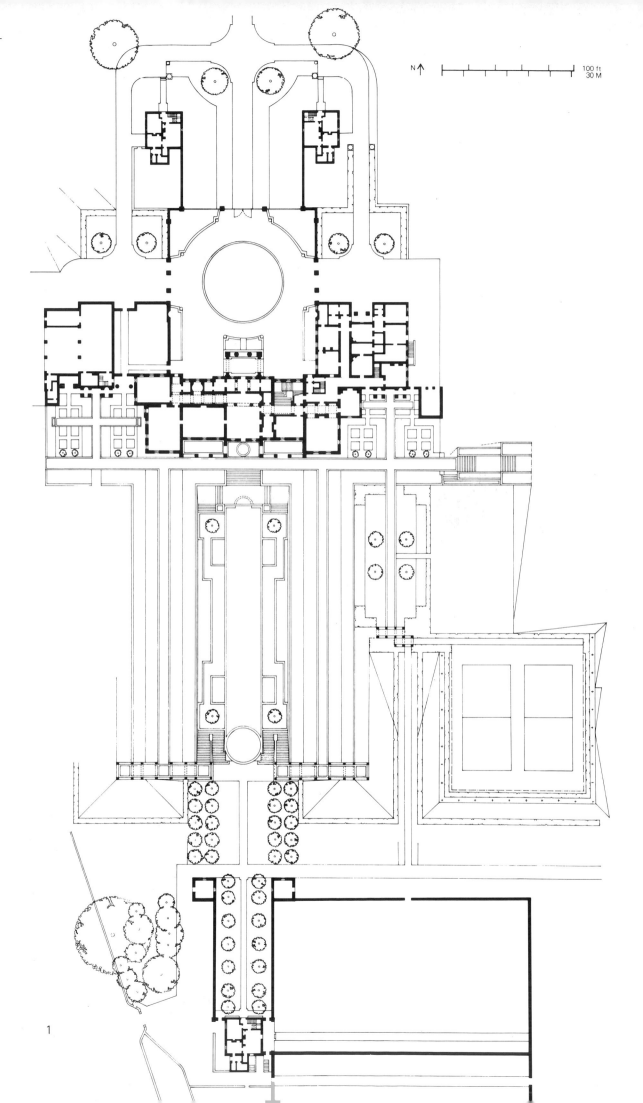

N↑   100 ft
      30 M

1

2

Gledstone Hall
1922-25
Yorkshire

Compared to Great Maytham or Nashdom, Gledstone is not a large building but the size of this stone house is deceptive. The incorporation of the lodges, forecourt, gardens and cottages with the house gives it a considerable scale, but this is contradicted by the domesticity of the garden elevation set under a large, hipped roof of stone slates and the subordination of the house to its terraced garden.

The relationship of the house to the forecourt and terraces is considerably influenced by Lutyens' arrangement of the Viceroy's House, New Delhi, and is contemporary with the gardens he added to Tyringham House, which are also concerned with the theme of a canal contained by the house, leading the eye along its length to a distant view of the countryside beyond. The gardens were planted by Gertrude Jekyll—then well into her eighties.

1 Plan
2 The north forecourt seen from the lodges (CL 1935)
3 Looking back from the pergola to the south front (CL 1935)

3

The Salutation
1911
Sandwich, Kent

The complexity of plan of the house and garden, the large, hipped roof and gigantic chimney-stacks are completely un-eighteenth century, even though the house is Queen Anne in style and built in two shades of red brick with stone quoins. The service wing is articulated as a single-storey extension and on the north side the cubic mass of the house is cut above the ground-floor level to allow windows to light the large staircase concealed in the centre of the building.

At the end of the village street a wide gateway with a roof on a deep plaster cornice spanning the gap between two outbuildings and contained by a pair of dormer windows forms a picturesque entrance. The house is set off axis and a route marked by three additional brick gateways extends the entrance axis through the gardens crossing the south lawn which is raised to the level of the reception rooms.

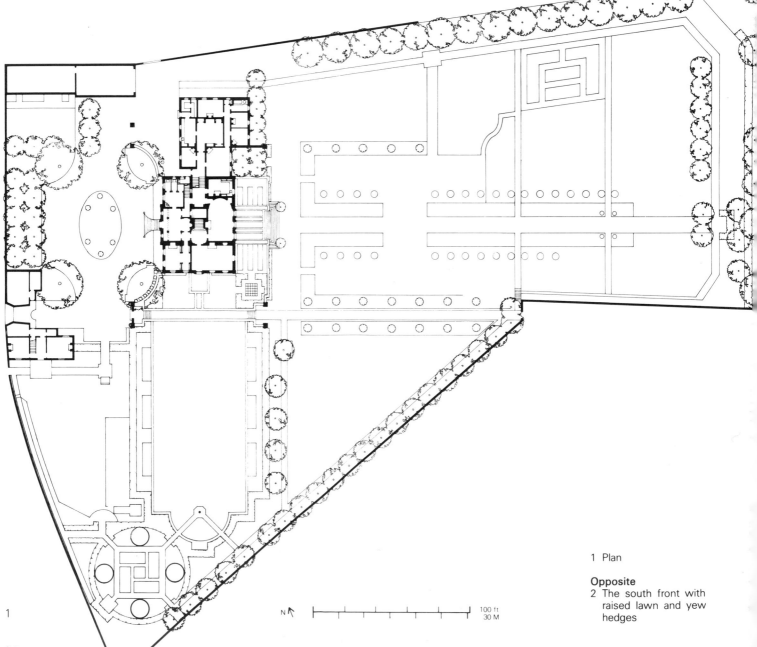

1

N

100 ft
30 M

1 Plan

Opposite
2 The south front with raised lawn and yew hedges

4

5

Opposite

3 East front showing the sundial which relates the otherwise severe facade to the garden

4 The route from the entrance lodge passes the south elevation and pairs of gateways and steps acknowledge entry to the raised south lawn (CL 1913)

5 The central staircase (CL 1962)

List of Buildings and Projects

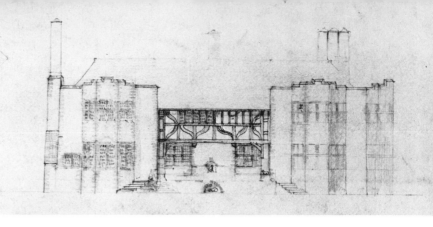

1

ENGLAND

Berkshire
1895-97 Binfield Lodge, Newbury:
        alterations for Capt Ernest Rhodes
1901   Deanery Garden, Sonning:
        house for E. Hudson, 1912 additions
1901   Folly Farm, Sulhampstead:
        addition for H. Cochrane, 1906 further
        additions, 1912 additions for Zachary
        Merton
1902   Sonning on Thames: proposal for a
        bridge
c.1902 Rush Court: proposed country house
1917   Basildon: proposal for a village layout,
        war memorial and church for Major
        J. A. Morrison (Park Farm Cottage,
        Basildon and cottages at Westridge
        Green constructed 1920-21)
1918   Basildon Park: alterations for Major
        J. A. Morrison
1921   Queen Mary's Dolls House Windsor
        Castle
1936   King George V Memorial, Windsor
1937   Tomb of King George V and Queen
        Mary St George's Chapel, Windsor
        Castle

Buckinghamshire
1893   Woodside, Chenies: garden layout for
        Adeline, Duchess of Bedford
1903   Pollard's Wood, Chalfont St Giles:
        house for Archibald Grove
1903   Chicheley Hall: proposed alterations for
        Sir George Farrer
1905-09 Nashdom, Taplow: house for Prince
        and Princess Alexis Dolgorouki
1913   Chalfont Park, Gerrards Cross:
        gardens and gardener's cottage for
        Mrs Edgar
1924   Beechwood, Slough: alterations for
        Hon Cecil Baring
1924-28 Tyringham House: gardens, temple of
        music and bathing pavilion
        for F. A. König
1933   Finch-Hatton Memorial Bridge:
        Eton College
1937   Passenham Manor, Stony Stratford:
        alterations for G. Ansley
1938   Filgrave School, Filgrave:
        clock tower given by F. A. König for
        George VI's coronation
      * Beaconsfield: proposed Romansque
        chapel for J. L. Garvin

Cambridgeshire
1908   Middlefield, Great Shelford:
        house for Henry Bond
c.1910 Gonville and Caius College, Cambridge:
        designs for screen in hall
1916   St Edmund's House, Cambridge:
        conversion of room to chapel
c.1922 Clare College, Cambridge:
        proposals for a memorial court
1924   Trinity College, Cambridge:
        proposal for a memorial garden and
        pavilion
1931-32 Benson Court, Magdalene College,
        Cambridge: part executed

Cornwall
c.1910 Looe: proposed hotel
1920   Penheale Manor, Egloskerry:
        additions for Capt P. Colville

Cheshire
1891   Eaton Hall: garden and temple for Duke
        of Westminster,
        1896-98 Italian Garden
1897   17-23 Corniche Road, Port Sunlight:
        cottages for W. H. Lever (Viscount
        Leverhulme)

Derbyshire
1907   Repton School: house for Mr L. A. Burd
1909   Renishaw Hall, Chesterfield:
        alterations for Sir George Sitwell
1912-13 Ednaston Manor: house and farm
        buildings for W. G. Player
1914-20 Renishaw Park Golf Club:
        extension of farmhouses to form
        clubhouse for Sir George Sitwell
1916   The Green, Eckington:
        garden for Sir George Sitwell

Devon
1909   Tavistock and Milton Abbott:
        estate cottages for the Duke of Bedford
1909   Milton Abbott: proposals, inn and water
        tower for the Duke of Bedford
1910-14 Littlecourt, Tavistock: house
        for Major Gallie
1910-30 Castle Drogo, Drewsteignton:
        house for Julius Drewe
1923   Mothecombe House, Yealmpton:
        additions for A. Mildmay
1932   Saunton Court: additions for G. Rankin
1934   Drum Inn, Cockington:
        inn for Cockington Village Trust

1 Overstrand Hall, Norfolk,
1899 — interest in
symmetry and
fortification overlay a
picturesque courtyard
scheme (BAL/RIBA
1899)

This chronology has been
derived from those included
in Butler's *The Architecture
of Sir Edwin Lutyens,*
Weaver's *Houses and
Gardens by Sir Edwin
Lutyens RA,* and the Catalogue of the *Drawings
Collection of the Royal
Institute of British Architects: Lutyens* compiled by
Margaret   Richardson,
together with research by
Peter Inskip.
The entries marked * are of
dates unknown to the
authors. War memorials
and personal memorial
tablets have been
omitted.

2

3

4

Crooksbury House, Surrey
2 1898 — Wrennaissance addition of east wing (CL 1900)
3 1914 — View from south — east wing remodelled with roughcast elevations under a hip roof. A picturesque chimney-stack softens the transition to the original house (CL c. 1920)
4 Gate in screen wall 1898 (CL c.1920)

Dorset
1927	Weston House, West Lulworth: house for Sir Alfred Fripp
1931	Fleet House, Fleet: reconstruction of eighteenth-century house for Mrs Saxton Noble

Essex
1894	Jekylls, Great Warley: garden layout for Miss E. Willmott
1900	Eastern Lodge: additions to cottage for the Countess of Warwick
1915	Grange Court, Chigwell: alterations for Hon C. Baring
	Gidea Park: proposed church

Gloucestershire
1901-02	Abbotswood, Lower Swell: additions and gardens for M. Fenwick
1906	Copse Hill House, Upper Slaughter: alterations to house and eight new cottages for Capt H. Brassey
1906	Stonehouse Court: alterations for A. S. Winterbottom
1920-21	Miserden Park: four-storey east wing addition for Noel Willis

Hampshire
1890	Little Tangley: stables for Cowley Lambert
1896	Micheldever: cottages and shops for the Earl of Northbrook
1897-08	Berrydown, Ashe: house and stables for A. Grove
1901-04	Marshcourt, Kings Somborne, near Stockbridge: house for Herbert Johnson, 1905 stables, 1924-26 great room added
1901	Old Basing Brickfields, Basing: cottage for Walter Hoare, c. 1905 office building
1903	Daneshill, Old Basing: house for Walter Hoare
1906	New Place, Shedfield: house for Mrs A. S. Franklin
1919	Cenotaph, Southampton
1923	Amport House: terraces, gatepiers and unexecuted pavilion for Mrs Sofer Whitburn
*	The Priory, Isle of Wight: extension to an eighteenth-century building

Herefordshire
1900	The Den, Pershore: garden for H. Avery

Hertfordshire
1896	Apsely End, Hemel Hempstead: four cottages and wheelwright's shop for Arthur Longham
1900	Knebworth: golf clubhouse
1900	Knebworth: cottages on the Earl of Lytton's estate
1901	Knebworth House: alterations for the Earl of Lytton, 1908 further alterations
1901	Homewood, Knebworth: house for the Dowager Lady Lytton
c.1908	Beacon House, Knebworth: house
1908-11	Temple Dinsley, Preston near Hitchin: alterations and extensions to house, new farm buildings and cottages for H. G. Fenwick, 1919 further extension to house, and new agent's house at Crunnells Green for Douglas Vickers
1912	Hill End, Hitchin: house for Mrs H. G. Fenwick
1914	Shenley Hill House: new billiard room for Mr S. de la Rue
1915	Church of St Martin, Knebworth
1922	Ashwell Bury: alterations for Mrs Fordham

Kent
1891-93	Plaxtol Church: proposed rebuilding of East End as memorial to M. Dalison
1903	Buckhurst, Withyham: alterations for R. H. Benson
1907-09	Great Maytham, Rolvenden: remodelling of eighteenth-century house and new cottages and stables for the Rt Hon H. J. Tennant
1907	Wittersham House: remodelling for Rt Hon A. Lyttleton
1909	Otford: church hall for Rev Mr Lutyens
1911	The Salutation, Sandwich: house for H. Farrer
1912	Knowlton Court: entrance lodge and remodelling of drawing room for Elmer Speed
1912	Barham Court: additions for E. Stainton
1913	Addington Park: proposed terrace and gardens for Mrs Sofer Whitburn
1925	Foxbury, Sevenoaks: alterations for Sir John Lloyd
1926	The Grange, Plaxtol: additions for M. Dalison
*	Calehill, near Ashford: preliminary designs for a house

5

Lancashire

1901 Rossal Beach: proposals for a seaside garden village for T. B. Lumb, (one house in Cross Way, lodges and four adjacent cottages in Way Gate executed)

1913 Abbey House, Barrow-in-Furness: chairman's house and gardener's cottage for Messrs Vickers

1923 Cenotaph, St Peter's Square, Manchester

1929-32 Midland Bank, King Street, Manchester: office building (with Whitney Son and Austin Hall)

1929-41 Metropolitan Cathedral of Christ the King, Liverpool: only crypt executed

* Midland Hotel, Windmill Street, Manchester: project for the hotel

Leicestershire

1903 Papillon Hall: house remodelling for F. Belville

1905 Thorpe Satchville Hall: entrance gates

1910 Lowesby Hall. alterations for Capt H. Brassey

London

1891 Wetherby Place: studio for F. Lutyens

1898 St John's Church, Smith Square: proposed rebuilding for Archdeacon Wilberforce

1899 94, Eaton Place: alterations for Mrs Cavan Irving

1899-05 St John's Institute, Tufton Street: parish hall for Archdeacon Wilberforce

1901 Vaudeville Theatre: scenery for 'Quality Street'

1901 Frognal Presbyterian Church, Finchley Road: competition entry

1901 1, Fitzjohn's Avenue: alterations for F. Debenham

1902 11, Stanhope Place: alterations for E. Stainton

1902 Berkeley Hotel, Piccadilly: alterations, 1913 grill room decoration

1902 10, Buckingham Street, alterations for the Earl of Lytton

1903-04 Tower House, Southampton Street: street clock for George Newnes Ltd

1903 7, Petersham Terrace: alterations for Adam Black

1904 2-10, Tavistock Street: *Country Life* building for Sir George Newnes

1905 Queens House, Chelsea: alterations for Jacques Blumenthal

1906 28, Queen Anne's Gate: alterations for Viscount Haldane

1906 15, Queen Anne's Gate: alterations for E. Hudson

1906 42, Kingsway: offices for 'The Garden' for W. Robinson

1906 51, Berkeley Square: alterations for Sir Basil Montgomery

1907 32, Queen Anne's Gate: alterations for Lady Allendale

1908 County Hall: competition entry

1908 10, Connaught Place: alterations for Lady Battersea

1908-20 Hamstead Garden Suburb: Church of St Jude on the Hill, Free Church, vicarage and manse, houses in Central Square, Erskine Hill and North Square

1909 16, Lower Berkeley Street: alterations for Sir John Horner

1910 Hanover Lodge, Regent's Park: alterations for Admiral Beatty

1910 100, Cheyne Walk: garden for Sir Hugh Lane

1911 Theosophical Society (now BMA), Tavistock Square and Burton Street, extended in 1923

1911 7, St James Square: house for G. and H. Farrer

1911-12 Roehampton House: alterations and additions for A. M. Grenfell

1911 Inner Temple: panelling to the Parliament Chamber

1911 Corner House, Cowley Street and 8, Little College Street: for Lady Norman and Hon F. Maclaren

1911 26a, Bryanston Square: alterations for Hon Cecil Baring

1912 36, Smith Square: house for Rt Hon Reginald McKenna

1912 18, Little College Street, house for Hon Alfred Lyttleton

1912 22, Bruton Street: alterations for M. Fenwick

1912 Shakespeare's England Exhibition, Earl's Court

1913 28, Portman Square: alterations for A. Mildmay

1913 Second Church of Christ Scientist, Palace Gardens Terrace: proposed church

c.1914 University of London: proposals for the Senate House

1914 74, Portland Place: alterations for

Hestercombe, Somerset
5 Gardens 1904 — a sequence of room-like spaces. Much of Lutyens' domestic work is anticipated in his garden designs

6   7   8

6   Hampstead Garden
Suburb, London, 1910
Houses in Central Square
— paradoxical
combination of both
scale and style (CL
c.1913)

7   Great Dixter, Sussex —
re-erection and extension
of 15th century house —
stone, brick and timber
construction imply
geological stratification
(CL c.1913)

8   Castle Drogo, Devon —
construction photograph
c.1914 (from the
collection of Anthony
Drewe)

	H. Philipson
1914	Golders Green Crematorium: mausoleum for the Philipson family
1914	Fleet Street: proposed offices for United Newspapers
1917	Adelphi Terrace: alterations for Sir James Barrie
1918	Wimborne House, Arlington Street: proposed entrance lodge for Viscount Wimborne
1918	20, New Cavendish Street: alterations for H. Pennoyer
1918	34, Hill Street: reconstruction for Lady Sackville
1918	182, Ebury Street: alterations and garden pavilion for Lady Sackville
1918	Bell House, Dulwich: alterations for Lady Lucas
1918	96, Cheyne Walk: alterations for Lady Cooper
1919	The Cenotaph, Whitehall
c.1920	1, King William Street: proposed offices for the London Assurance Company
c.1920	8, Great George Street: proposed offices for Armstrong-Whitworth
1920-24	Britannic House, Finsbury Circus, offices for the Anglo-Iranian Oil Company
c.1920	8, Bishopsgate: alterations for Baring Bros
1921	43, Green Street: alterations for P. Vaughan Morgan
1922	Midland Bank, 196, Piccadilly
1922	Devonshire House, Piccadilly: proposed office development
1922	11, Carlton House Terrace: alterations for B. Guinness
1922	104, Eaton Square: alterations for Capt O. Lyttleton
1923	35, Lowndes Square: alterations for Rt Hon Sir Alfred Mond, MP
1923	7, Clarendon Place: alterations for General B. Freyburg, VC
1924	British Empire Exhibition, Wembley: pavilion for *The Times*
1924	St James' Park: proposals for a new stone bridge
1924-39	Midland Bank, Poultry: head office (with Gotch and Saunders)
1924	Warwick House, Norfolk Street: alterations for Capt E. Wallace, MP
1924	43, Bryanston Square: alterations for Sir George Lewis
1925	18, Buckingham Gate: alterations for

	Lady Apsley
1925	29, Belgrave Square: alterations for Mrs Harris Lebus
1926	Mercantile Marine War Memorial, Tower Hill
1926-28	Grosvenor House, Park Lane: elevations (with Wimperis, Simpson and Guthrie)
1927	Euston Station: decorations for the hall
1927	Terminal House, Grosvenor Gardens: elevations
1928-29	67-68, Pall Mall: elevations for V. Behar (with Romaine-Walker and Jenkins)
1928	Midland Bank, Leadenhall Street
1928-33	Hampton Court: new bridge for Middlesex and Surrey County Councils
1928	29, Hyde Park Gate: alterations for Sir Roderick Jones
1928	YWCA Building, Great Russell Street
1929-31	120, Pall Mall: offices for Crane Bennett Ltd
1929-30	Page Street: housing for Westminster City Council
1929-33	British Industries House and Hereford House, Oxford Street: elevations
1929	117, Eaton Square: alterations for the Earl of Kenmare
1929	4, Connaught Place: alterations for Capt O. Lyttleton
1929	Charing Cross: proposed bridge
1930	Alford House, Park Lane: elevational consultant
1930	66, Lincolns Inn Fields: restoration of façade for Farrer and Co
1930-33	42, Cheyne Walk: house for Hon Mrs Guy Liddell
1931	11, Connaught Place: alterations for T. J. Ley
1932	Brook House, Park Lane: façades (with W. B. Simpson)
1934	5, Balfour Place: alterations for Mrs Louis Lebus
1935	36, Hill Street: conversion of mews for Baroness Porcelli
1935	85 Fleet Street: Reuter's and Press Association HQ (with Smee and Houchin)
1936	Salisbury Court: 'The Codgers' public house
1936	Greenwich Maritime Museum: elliptical room for Sir James Caird
1937	16, Stafford Place: alterations for Rt Hon Leslie Hore-Belish, MP
1937	Thurloe Place: proposed National Theatre

9　　　　　　　　10　　　　　　　　　　11

1937	Coronation Ball, Albert Hall: scenery
1938	Ranelagh: proposed housing for V. Behar
1938	Ranelagh Club, Fulham: proposed polo club
1938	Tower Hill: scheme for layout
1939	Trafalgar Square: fountains
1940	Royal Academy London: planning committee
1942	South Bank: proposed National Theatre
1942	Westminster Abbey: suggested Gothic narthex
*	The Bishop's Avenue: proposed house for Lady Sackville
*	29, Belgrave Square: staircase alterations
*	Rutland House, Knightsbridge: proposed interior decoration
*	Audley House, 8, 9 and 10, North Audley Street: façades for the Grosvenor Estate, executed by George Stewart
*	White City Stadium: proposals

Middlesex
1926　Bell Weir Bridge, Staines: executed 1959

Norfolk
1898　Nonconformist Chapel, Overstrand
1899　The Pleasuance, Overstrand: alterations for Lord Battersea
1899-01　Overstrand Hall: house for Lord Hillingdon
pre 1908　Overstrand: project for a house for Sir George Alexander
1918　Breccles Hall: alterations for Rt Hon E. Montagu, MP

Northamptonshire
1897　East Haddon Hall: gardens for C. Guthrie
1904-38　Ashby St Ledger's: extensive alterations for Hon Ivor Guest (Lord Wimborne)

Northumberland
1903　Lindisfarne Castle, Holy Island: reconstruction for E. Hudson
c.1905　Holy Trinity Church, Berwick on Tweed: reredos
1907　Angerton, Morpeth: gardens for F. Straker
1908-09　Whalton Manor: conversion of four

houses into one for Mrs E. Smith
1909　Meldon Park: proposals for lodges for Col Cookson, 1937 alterations to house
1937-38　Blagdon Hall: garden and proposed swimming pool for Viscount Ridley

Nottinghamshire
1913　Nottingham: proposed offices for the Imperial Tobacco Company

Oxfordshire
1935　Christchurch, Oxford: pool in Tom Quad
1935-37　Campion Hall, Brewer Street, Oxford: quadrangle for the Society of Jesus, (part executed)
1938　Middleton Park, Middleton Stoney: house and lodges for Lord Jersey

Somerset
1900　Church of St Peter and St Paul, Kilmersdon: lych gate for Lord Hylton
1901　Redlynch House: east wing added for the Earl of Ilchester
1901　Mells Manor House: restoration for Sir John Horner, 1904 alterations
1902　Ammerdown House: garden for Lord Hylton
1904　Hestercombe House: orangery and gardens for Hon E. W. Portman
1925　Church of St Nicholas, Brushford: memorial chapel
1925　Mells Park House: house for R. McKenna

Suffolk
1897-99　Stoke College, Stoke by Clare: additions for Lord Loch
1901　St Peter's House, Ipswich: almshouse for C. H. Berners
1902　Dalham Hall: proposed additions, 1906 lodge and entrance for Col Rhodes
1923　Mesnil Warren, Newmarket: alterations for Hon G. Lambton
1933-34　Brent Eleigh Hall: additions for H. Pennoyer

Surrey
1888　The Corner, Thursley: conversion of row of cottages into a house for E. Gray, 1890 additions for C. D. Heatley, 1895 two further wings
1889　Park Hatch, Hoe Farm, Hascombe: lodges for J. Goodman

Viceroy's House, New Delhi, 1922 — '...temporal power... hedged with the divinity of earthly splendour' (Architectural Review Jan 1931)
9　The main entrance (CL)
10　South approach (CL)

11　Palace for HH the Maharajah of Kashmir, New Delhi, 1919 (BAL/RIBA 1919)

12

13

14

Architect to Imperial War
Graves Commission:
12 The Cenotaph,
Whitehall, London,
1919 (CL)
13 The Cenotaph and
Great War Stone,
Manchester,
Lancashire, 1923
14 The Memorial to the
Missing, Thiepval,
France, 1923 (CL)

1889	Littleworth, Seale: gardener's cottage for H. A. Mangles
1889-91	Crooksbury House: house and outbuildings for A. W. Chapman, 1898 new east wing, 1902 stables and gardens, 1914 alterations of façades for new owner, F. E. Biggs
1892	Shere: lych gate for Sir Reginald Bray, Shere Church
1892	Shere: cottages and shops for Sir Reginald Bray
1892	The Red House, Effingham: house for Miss Susan Muir-Mackenzie
1893-95	Chinthurst Hill, Wonersh: house for Miss Amelia Guthrie
1894	The Hut, Munstead: cottage for Gertrude Jekyll
1894	Manor House, Shere: lodge for Sir Reginald Bray
1894	Ruckmans, Oakwood Park: additions for Miss Lyell, 1902 music room extension
1895	Northbrook, Hurtmore Road, Godalming: dairy
1896	Sullingstead, Hascombe: house for C. A. Crook, 1903 music room extension
1896	Munstead Wood: house for Gertrude Jekyll
1897-99	Orchards, Munstead: house for Sir William Chance
1897	Woodend, Witley: alterations for Lady Stewart
1897	Farnham: Liberal club
1897	Fulbrook House: house for G. Streatfield
1897	Hazelhatch, Burrows Cross: alterations for Hon E. Lawless
1898	Church of St John the Baptist, Busbridge: chancel screen
1898	Munstead House: alterations and orangery for Sir Herbert Jekyll
1898	Witwood, Camberley: new house
1899	Goddards, Abinger Common: almshouse for Sir Frederick Mirrieless, 1910 extended and adapted into a house
1899	Post office, Abinger
1899	Littlecroft, Guildford: house for Mrs Bowes Watson
1899	The Red House, Frith Hill Road, Godalming: house for Rev W. H. Evans
1899	Tigbourne Court, Witley: house for E. Horne
1900	Institute, Thursley

1900	Rake Manor, Milford: additions for Mrs Cavan Irving
1900	Fisher's Hill, Woking: house for Rt Hon Gerald Balfour, MP, 1907 Fisher's Hill cottage
1901	Holmwood, Dorking: alterations for Wildman Catley
1901	Warren Lodge, Thursley: cottages for R. W. Webb, 1909 alterations to Warren Lodge
1902	Furnace Farm (now Summer Farm), Clandon: house for Arthur Wood
1902	Great Holt, Frensham: proposed additions for Major Boyce Combe
1903	Church of St Martin, Pixham, Dorking: sanctuary, church room and proposed tower for Miss M. Mayo
1903	The Mount School, Hindhead: new house for W. G. Jackson
1904	Millmead, Bramley: house for Gertrude Jekyll
1904	La Mascot: house for F. W. Pethick-Lawrence
1905	Esher Palace: sunken garden for Lady Helen Vincent
1906	Pasture Wood, Dorking: gardens for Miss F. Mirrieless
1906	The Dormy House, Walton Heath Golf Club: clubhouse for G. A. Riddell
1908	Chussex, Walton Heath: house for W. H. Fowler
1913	Frog's Island, Walton Heath: additions for the Countess of Londesborough
1916-17	Felbridge: proposed large house
1930	Egham Memorial Lodges, Runnymede: for Lady Fairhaven
1931	Guildford: bridge over Pilgrim's Way
1933-34	North House, Prince's Way, Wimbledon: house and lodge for R. Wilson Black
1934	The Cedar House, Chobham: house for W. H. Colt
c.1935	Parkwood, Englefield Green: designs for entrance gate and library for W. L. Baillieu
1937	Colley Lane, Reigate: cricket pavilion and pavilion cottages for Sir William Mallinson
1943	Brockham Green: book production works for Mr Mackintosh
*	The Old House, Pyrford: proposed new entrance

15   16   17   18

Sussex

1894	Lascombe, Puttenham: alterations for Col Spencer
1898	Gravetye Manor: proposed alterations for W. Robinson
1898	Rowfant: alterations for Mr Locke Lampson
1899	Mayfield: house for Rev A. Wickham
1902	Little Thakeham, Thakeham: house for E. Blackburn
1902	The Hoo, Willingdon: additions and gardens for A. Wedderburn, KC
1903	Monkton House, Singleton: house for W. James
1905	Eartham House: remodelling for Sir William Bird
1905	Forest House, Forest Row: alterations for Miss Hale
1906	Barton St Mary, East Grinstead: house for Sir G. Munro Miller
1910	Great Dixter, Northiam: enlargement of fifteenth-century house for Nathaniel Lloyd
1911	Osgoods, Capel: additions
1913	Brede Place: additions for Moreton Frewen
1918	40 Sussex Square, Brighton: alterations for Lady Sackville
1919	The Grange, Rottingdean: remodelling for Sir George Lewis
c.1920	Legh Manor, Cuckfield: alterations for Lady Chance
1923	White Lodge-on-the-Cliff, Roedean: additions and proposed colonnade for Lady Sackville
1927	Plumpton Place: footbridge, cottages, lodges, approach and gardens for E. Hudson
1927	Mill House, Plumpton: restoration for E. Hudson
1928	Marvells, Five Ashes: cottage for G. Plank
193	Halnaker House, near Chichester: house for Rt Hon R. McKenna

Warwickshire

| 1900 | Myton Sand: proposed house for Lady Warwick |
| 1919-21 | Clifford Manor, Clifford Chambers, near Stratford-upon-Avon: restoration for Mrs Rees-Mogg |

Yorkshire

| 1905 | Esholt, Sheffield: gardens for |

A. J. Hobson

1905-07	Heathcote, King's Road, Ilkley: house for E. Hemingway
1922-25	Gledstone Hall: house for Sir Amos Nelson (with Richard Jacques)
1929	York: offices for NE Railway Co
1937	Midland Bank, Leeds: proposed offices Houghton Hall: garden

SCOTLAND

1896	The Ferry Inn, Rosneath, Dunbarton: two wings added to existing inn for Princess Louise, Duchess of Argyll.
1898	Dunbarton, Rosneath House: alterations for Princess Louise
1900	Gullane, East Lothian: Grey Walls, house for Rt Hon Alfred Lyttleton, 1909 lodges for William James
1929	Stornoway, Outer Hebrides: proposed hotel for Sir William Lever

WALES

| 1923-24 | Newport, Monmouthshire: waterworks filtration plant |

IRELAND

1906-07	Heywood House, County Leix: gardens and fountains for Sir E. Hucheson Poe
1905-12	Lambay Castle, County Dublin: restoration and extensions for Hon C. Baring (Lord Revelstoke), 1909 garden, 1916 proposed chapel, 1922 tomb, double house, farm buildings and cottages, 1932 guest house
1910	Howth Castle, County Dublin: additions and restoration for J. Gaisford- St Lawrence
1912	Dublin: proposed art gallery over River Liffey for Sir Hugh Lane
1930-33	Islandbridge, Dublin: Park of Remembrance, Irish National War Memorial

BELGIUM

| 1928 | Antwerp Exhibition, British pavilion |

EAST GERMANY

| * | Meiningen Hospital, Meiningen: director's house |

The move to 'Elementalism':
15 Midland Bank, Picadilly, London, 1922 (CL)
16 Midland Bank, Head Office, Poultry, London, 1924 (CL)
17 Midland Bank, Manchester, Lancashire, 1929 (CL)
18 Metropolitan Roman Catholic Cathedral, Liverpool, Lancashire, 1929 (CL)

Munstead Wood, Munstead, Surrey 1896. The gables
of the garden front are reminiscent of Voysey's work ▶

Berrydown Court, Ashe, Overton, Hampshire 1897-8.
The garden front is broken down into three different
elements

19

20

21

Continuation of earlier
idioms:
Classical
19 Middleton Park,
     Oxford, 1938 (CL)
20 Middleton Park,
     Oxford, 1938 (CL)
Vernacular
21 Halnaker House,
     Sussex, 1938 (CL)

FRANCE

1898	Le Bois des Moutiers, Varengeville: additions and remodelling for G. Mallet
1898	Clos du Dan, Varengeville: proposed house for G. Mallet
1898-99	Paris Exhibition of 1900: designs for the British pavilion
c.1908	Hotel proposal for north coast
1909	Les Communes, Varengeville: house for G. Mallet
1912-13	Ranguin, Grasse: alterations and additions to a house for G. Mallet
1917-18	The Great War Stone for the Imperial War Graves Commission
1918-20	Etaples: war memorial and cemetery
1918-20	Gezaincourt, Somme: communal cemetery extension
1918-20	La Neuville, Corbie: British cemetery
1920	The Great War Cross for the Imperial War Graves Commission
1923-30	Thiepval: war memorial and cemetery to the missing of the Somme
1924-38	Villers-Bretonneux, Somme: Australian war memorial
1925-28	Arras: memorial to the missing of the Royal Air Force
post 1926	St Hilaire: proposed house for Col Ganet

HUNGARY

1905	Bodrog Olaszi, Zemplen: alterations for Count Elemer Lonyay

ITALY

1910	Rome Exhibition of 1912: British pavilion, 1912-16 pavilion converted into the British School
1911	Turin: Exhibition pavilion

INDIA

New Delhi

1912	Viceroy's house
1912	Jaipur column
c.1912	Official bungalows
1917	Proposed cathedral
1919	Anthropological museum: depository for Sir Aurel Stein's collection of frescoes
1919	Proposed palace for HH the Maharajah of Kashmir
1920	Proposed little palace for HH the Maharajah of Bikanir
1921	Palace for HH the Gaekwar of Baroda
1922	Proposed medical research institute
1922-25	Record office and proposed war museum
1923-30	Proposed house for HH the Jam Sahib of Nawanagar
1924	All India War Memorial Arch
1926	Fountains flanking Jaipur column
1926	Palace for the Nizan of Hyderbad
1930	King George V Memorial
1939	Proposed court of justice
*	House for Bahadur Lala Sultan Singh

Rest of India

1916	Baroda: library for the Maharajah Gaekwar of Baroda
1918	Alwar: acted as consultant for the town plan for the Maharajah of Alwar
1920	Lucknow: proposed university
1924	Bavendra Palace, Jamnagar: gardens
1937-38	Jaipur: proposed processional archway for the Maharajah of Jaipur

SPAIN

1915-28	El Guadalperal, Elgordo, Toledo: designs and preliminary work for a new palace for the Duke of Penaranda
1917	Ventosilla, near Toledo: reconstruction of a farmhouse for the Duke of Santona
1920	El Guadalperal: proposed smaller palace for the Duke of Penaranda
1939-42	Palacio de Liria, Madrid: restoration scheme for the Duke of Alba executed by Cabanes between 1950 and 1955

SOUTH AFRICA

1909	Pretoria: suggested alterations to Sir Herbert Baker's Union Building
1910-20	Capetown: proposals for university
1910	Johannesburg: art gallery, 1929 extension to art gallery, 1936 new wing to art gallery
1910	Johannesburg: Proposed church

USA

1903	New York: proposed house on the Hudson River for S. Harriman
1925	Washington DC: British Embassy

Bibliography

Writings by Sir Edwin Lutyens

'The Work of the late Philip Webb', *Country Life*, vol. 37, 1915, p. 619.

'What I think of Modern Architecture', *Country Life*, vol. 69, 1931, pp. 775-7.

'On Modern Architecture', *Architectural Review*, vol. 54, December 1923, pp. xlii-xliv.

Writings by others

BETJEMAN, JOHN, 'Memorial to a Great Architect', *Country Life*, vol. 109, February 2, 1951, pp. 324-5.

BINNEY, MARCUS, 'An Architecture of Law and Order', *Country Life*, vol. 145, April 10, 1969, pp. 826-7.

GREENBERG, ALAN, 'Lutyens' Architecture Re-studied', *Yale Perspecta*, vol. 12, 1969, pp. 129-52.

GOODHART-RENDEL, H., 'Sir Edwin Lutyens OM, PRA', *RIBA Journal*, vol. 51, January 1944, pp. 51-3.

——— 'Lutyens and His Work', *The Builder*, vol. 168, February 16, 1945, pp. 127-31.

——— 'The Work of the late Sir Edwin Lutyens OM', *RIBA Journal*, vol. 52, March 1945, pp. 123-9.

HILL, OLIVER, 'Review of the Memorial Volumes', *The Builder*, vol. 181, October 26, 1951, pp. 546-9.

——— 'The Genius of Edwin Lutyens', *Country Life*, vol. 145, March 27, 1969, pp. 710-12.

HASLING, G., 'Liverpool Metropolitan Cathedral: A Comparison of the Scott and Lutyens Designs', *The Builder*, vol. 188, March 4, 1955, pp. 366-8.

HUSSEY, CHRISTOPHER, 'The Personality of Sir Edwin Lutyens', *RIBA Journal*, vol. 76, April 1969, pp. 142-5.

——— Obituary, *Country Life*, vol. 95, 1944, pp. 68-71.

INSKIP, PETER, 'The Compromise of Castle Drogo', *Architectural Review*, vol. 165, April 1979, pp. 220-6.

LUTYENS, ROBERT, 'The Necessity for Lutyens', *Architect's Journal*, vol. 97, February 18, 1943, pp. 119-22.

——— 'The Genesis of Sir Edwin Lutyens', *Country Life*, vol. 112, November 28, 1952, pp. 1726-8.

PEVSNER, NIKOLAUS, 'Building with Wit, the Architecture of Sir Edwin Lutyens', *Architectural Review*, vol. 109, April 1951, pp. 217-25.

POLLEN, FRANCIS, 'The Genius of Edwin Lutyens – the Last of the Classicists', *Country Life*, vol. 145, April 3, 1969, pp. 794-6.

RICHARDSON, A. E., Obituaries, *The Builder*, CLXVI, 1944, *Building*, XIX, 1944, p. 32, *Architectural Review*, vol. 95, 1944, p. xiv.

SMITHSON, ALISON, 'The Responsibility of Lutyens', *RIBA Journal*, vol. 76, April 1969, pp. 146-51.

SMITHSON, PETER, 'The Viceroy's House in Imperial Delhi', *RIBA Journal*, vol. 76, April 1969, pp. 152-4.

STAMP, GAVIN, 'The Rise and Fall of Edwin Lutyens', *Architectural Review*, November 1981.

SUMMERSON, JOHN, 'The Lutyens Memorial Volumes', *RIBA Journal*, vol. 58, August 1951, pp. 390-1.

VENTURI, ROBERT AND SCOTT BROWN, DENISE, 'Learning from Lutyens', *RIBA Journal*, vol. 76, August 1969, pp. 353-4.

WRIGHT, FRANK LLOYD, 'Review of The Memorial Volumes', *Building*, July 1951, pp. 260-2.

BRANDON JONES, JOHN; HUSSEY, CHRISTOPHER; BAGNAL, HOPE; FURNEAUX JORDAN, R.; FARQUHARSON, HORACE; MILNE, O. P.; HANNEN, NICHOLAS; WORTHINGTON, SIR HUBERT; CURTIS GREEN, W.; SHOOSMITH, A. G.; MEDD, H.A.N.; AUSTEN HALL, H.; BUTLER, A.S.G., 'Reminiscences on Sir Edwin Lutyens' *AA Journal*, vol. 74, March 1959, pp. 226-36.

Books

BUTLER, A.S.G. with George Stewart and Christopher Hussey, *The Architecture of Sir Edwin Lutyens*, three volumes, London 1950.

FAWCETT, JANE (editor), article by R. Gradidge, *Seven Victorian Architects*, London 1976.

GRADIDGE, RODERICK, *Dream Houses: The Edwardian Ideal*, London 1980.

——— *Edwin Lutyens: Architect Laureate*, 1981.

HUSSEY, CHRISTOPHER, *The Life of Sir Edwin Lutyens*, three volumes, London 1950.

IRVING, ROBERT GRANT, *Indian Summer, The Making of New Delhi*, 1981.

JEKYLL, GERTRUDE, *Home and Garden*, London 1900.

LUTYENS, MARY, *Edwin Lutyens, A Memoir by his Daughter*, London 1980.

LUTYENS, ROBERT, *Sir Edwin Lutyens, An Appreciation in Perspective, by his Son*, London 1942.

——— *Six Great Architects*, London 1959.

O'NEILL, DANIEL, *Sir Edwin Lutyens: Country Houses*, London 1980.

RICHARDSON, MARGARET (compiled by), *Catalogue of the Drawings Collection of the Royal Institute of British Architects: Lutyens*, Farnborough 1973.

WEAVER, SIR LAWRENCE, *Houses and Gardens by Sir Edwin Lutyens RA*, London 1913, reprinted 1981.

Catalogue

Lutyens: The Work of the English Architect Sir Edwin Lutyens (1869-1944), Art Council of Great Britain, 1981.

Résumé en francais

Sir Edwin Landseer Lutyens est né en 1869. Exactement contemporain de Frank Lloyd Wright, il avait un an de moins que Mackintosh, et douze ans de moins que Voysey. Après une formation classique relativement courte sauf en ce qui concerne la période pendant laquelle il étudia avec Gertrude Jekyll l'architecture vernaculaire de chez lui, il fut engagé par Sir Ernest George. C'est seulement deux ans après qu'il ouvrit sa propre agence et, entre 1889 et 1912, il construisit un grand nombre de maisons remarquables. En 1912 à New Delhi on lui confia le projet de la maison du vice roi et il dessina un plan d'urbanisme ainsi que les plans de nombreux autres bâtiments. Simultanément, il travaillait sur de grandes constructions à usage commercial dans la Cité de Londres. Après la guerre 1914-18 il fut nommé architecte en chef de la commission impériale des cimetières de guerre, il dessina le Cenotaphe, le monument au soldat inconnu à Thiepval en France ainsi que de nombreux autres. Entre les deux guerres son agence prit de l'extension, et pendant la deuxième guerre mondiale, alors président de l'Académie Royale il fut chargé de la reconstruction de Londres après les bombardements. Il mourut en janvier 1944, achevant le projet de la cathédrale catholique romaine à Liverpool, un bâtiment destiné à rivaliser Saint Pierre par sa dimension et dont la construction fut finalement abandonnée en 1959 pour raisons financières, seule la crypte étant achevée.

L'essai analytique de Peter Inskip est concentré sur les maisons individuelles. Il s'attache tout d'abord aux diverses références de Lutyens; ses contemporains tels Norman Shaw, Philip Webb, et enfin, surtout Vanbrugh, Hawksmoor, Wren et Palladio. Les clients de Lutyens comme ceux de Shaw étaient des hommes décidés, autodidactes, qui dans l'ensemble respectaient leur architecte pour sa réussite.

Country Life fondé en 1897, publiait régulièrement les travaux de Lutyens, ce qui lui amena des clients admiratifs. Le programme de ses maisons développait le principe de la résidence secondaire à la campagne. *'Les plans de base des maisons de Lutyens sont généralement les mêmes, respectant l'intimité et le confort des hôtes par une division hiérarchique des pièces entre les hôtes, la famille et le service.'*

Pour presque chaque maison il semble évident que Lutyens cherche à augmenter les dimensions apparentes du bâtiment. Non seulement dans le détail de ses plans mais aussi dans l'organisation des circulations. La relation de la taille au volume, de la maison au jardin contribue à donner l'impression de grandeur. Le jardin en tant qu' extension de la maison . . . ne lui est pas subordonné. Quant à la relation maison-jardin on conçoit clairement son importance dans l'architecture de Lutyens. Ou bien la structure de la maison s'étend sur le site tout entier, ou bien les éléments du jardin sont traités en fortifications fictives de manière à isoler les terrasses de la campagne environnante et de toute les manières, il établit une unité entre la maison et le jardin. Il y a apparemment deux raisons: d'une part la volonté d'élargir énormément l'expérience de la maison et celle de préserver le cachet d'un endroit particulier. La plupart des concepts d'aménagement intérieurs s'appliquent au jardin. Nous remarquons, tandis que la structure des jardins en plan apparait identique à celle de la maison ce qui implique des volumes formés en galerie, que la volumétrie des jardins est différenciée par la formation de terrasses, par des plantations, des mûrets, des fontaines et des sculptures judicieusement placées . . .'

Après une analyse de Deanery Garden, Inskip écrit: *'La division hiérarchique des espaces sur le terrain est tout à fait comparable à celle qui existe dans un château Mediéval. Dans la plupart de ses premières maisons le Hall est utilisé comme élément dominant. Mais à Goddards (1899-1910) il utilise la cour extérieure en tant que volume principal, et à Lindisfarne, les niveaux supérieurs et inférieurs dominent un espace intérieur; ainsi progressivement Lutyens utilise les terrasses jardins comme point culminant autour duquel il organise ses maisons. Ceci est particulièrement vrai dans son utilisation fréquente des styles classiques. Quatre de ses maisons nous montrent cette progression: Little Thakeham (1902), Heathcote (1906), Great Maytham (1907) et Gledstone Hall (1922). Chaque plan est symétrique par rapport à un axe principal Nord Sud et comporte deux séquences linéaires identiques d'espaces indépendants —cour d'entrée, vestibule, hall et jardin. Little Thakeham et Heathcote tendent à utiliser le Hall en tant que point culminant du terrain plutôt que de la maison seule, alors que Great Maytham et Gledstone tendent à utiliser les jardins comme éléments dominants.'*

'Beaucoup des maisons de Lutyens présentent un caractère pompeux et monotone à cause du programme et de l'approche conceptuelle, cependant ses meilleures réalisations l'évitent en utilisant le paradoxe et souvent la jouissance de ces maisons repose sur une contradiction propre à la conception'. A l'intérieur ceci devient plus évident par le contraste qui oppose la somptuosité des volumes architecturaux avec la simplicité du mobilier et des couleurs, bien qu'il ne reste que peu de trâce à travers le brouillard de chintz qui recouvre la plupart des oeuvres. Les matériaux de construction étaient la plupart du temps choisis pour donner aux maisons l'apparence de l'ancien. Pour Lutyens l'apparente patine du temps est un facteur important dans l'évaluation esthétique.

Pour conclure avec la discussion de Homewood, Inskip observe que *'le paradoxe* soutend l'ensemble et unifie Homewood de la même façon que les éléments de géométrie unifient Heathcote. Bien qu'elle soit suggérée, la relation de la route à la propriété, l'approche des axes de circulation vers la maison, se révèle à moitié faite. La route principale est reléguée brusquement à la fonction d'une route secondaire. Un grand escalier dramatiquement éclairé aparaît en plein centre d'une sombre villa, plutôt dégarnie, une villa classique étonnamment dans un cottage, et un cottage d'architecture vernaculaire au milieu de terrasses classiques.'

Finalement nous pouvons dire que les expériences des maisons de Lutyens peuvent être dans de nombreux cas claustrophobiques. Elles sont si dépendantes de la fantaisie d'un monde illusoire qu'elles manquent de la spontanéité des solutions directes que Lutyens admirait tant dans les oeuvres de Philip Webb et dont il s'est tant inspiré en particulier pour Homewood. Sa décadence romantique serait plus appropriée pour la maison d'une comtesse douairière, l'intention d'agrandissement semble éventuellement grossir la maison jusqu'à l'hypertrophie et le monde hermétique des plaisanteries idiosyncratiques peut devenir précieux jusqu'à l'excès dans sa monotonie. Sans toutefois réussir à atteindre le radical changement conceptuel opéré par ses contemporains Américains et Européens, les maisons de Lutyens atteignent souvent dans leur tenue et dans les solutions architecturales qu'elles apportent un éclat largement au niveau de ses contemporains Anglais.'

Deutsche Zusammenfassung

Sir Edwin Landseer Lutyens wurde 1869 geboren, aufs Jahr ein Zeitgenosse von Frank Lloyd Wright, ein Jahr später als Mackintosh und 12 Jahre später als Voysey. Nach einer sehr kurzen Ausbildung — ausgenommen die Zeit mit Gertrude Jekyll, während der er die ortsübliche Bauweise rund um sein Zuhause in Surrey studierte — fängt er im Büro von Sir Ernest George an. Nur zwei Jahre später eröffnet er ein eigenes Büro und baut in den Jahren zwischen 1889 und 1912 eine große Zahl von hervorragenden Häusern. Im Jahr 1912 erhält er den Auftrag für das Haus des Vizekönigs in Neu Delhi, im Zusammenhang mit dem er einen Bebauungsplan mit vielen weiteren Gebäuden ausarbeitet. Gleichzeitig fängt er an, an großen Geschäftshäusern in der City von London zu arbeiten. Nach dem ersten Weltkrieg wird er oberster Architekt der Kommission für Kriegsgräber und entwirft den Cenotaph, die Gedenkstätte für die verlorene Schlacht von Thiepval in Frankreich und viele Kriegerdenkmäler. Zwischen den beiden Weltkriegen vergrößert sein Büro sein Aufgebenfeld. Und während des zweiten Weltkrieges, als er Präsident der Royal Academy wird, arbeitet er nach dem 'Blitz' Pläne für den Wiederaufbau von London aus. Er starb im Januar 1944, umgeben von seinen Zeichnungen für die römisch-katholische Kathedrale für Liverpool, ein Gebäude, das vom Maßstab her St. Peter in den Schatten stellen sollte, dessen Bau allerdings 1959 schließlich aus Kostengründen aufgegeben wurde, nach dem nur die Krypta fertiggestellt war.

Peter Inskips analytisches Essay widmet sich nur den Häusern. Er beginnt, indem er die verschiedenen Quellen aufzeigt, aus denen Lutyens angeregt worden war; von Zeitgenossen wie Norman Shaw, Philip Webb und schließlich von Vanbrugh, Hawksmoor, Wren und Palladio. Lutyens' Bauherren waren — ganz wie auch Shaws — unternehmungslustige selfmade men, die im großen Ganzen ihren Architekten um seines Erfolges willen respektieren. Obwohl im Falle Lutyens die Zeitschrift *Country Life*, im Jahr 1897 gegründet, durch regelmäßige Veröffentlichungen seines Werks ihm bewundernde Bauherren brachte.

Das Raumprogramm entwickelte sich um die Idee der Wochenendparty im Landhaus mit Besuchern, die über Nacht blieben. Im allgemeinen liegt Lutyens' Häusern derselbe Grundriß mit den gleichen Erfordernissen zugrunde, der die Privatsphäre und das Bedürfnis des Gastes nach Komfort respektiert und das Haus in einem hierarchischen Arrangement aufgliedert in Bereiche für Gästen, Familie und Personal.

In nahezu jedem Haus kann man Lutyens' Versuch, das tatsächliche Volumen des Hauses zu vergrößern, nachweisen. Dies zeigt sich nicht nur bei dem Entwurf der Details, sondern auch in der Art und Weise, wie Lutyens den Weg des Besuchers durch das Haus organisiert. Die Vergrößerung entsteht sowohl durch die Gestaltung der Massen, als auch vor allem durch die Beziehung von Haus zu Garten, der oft als integrale Erweiterung des Hauses selbst angesehen wird und nicht als ein untergeordnetes Element.

'Wenn man nun die Beziehung zwischen Haus und Garten betrachtet, kann man ganz deutlich sehen, daß dies von allerhöchster Wichtigkeit für Lutyens' Architektur ist. Entweder wird die geometrische Struktur des Hauses auf das ganze Grundstück ausgeweitet oder einzelne Gartenelemente werden als fiktive Befestigungsanlagen angesehen, die die Terrassen von der umgebenden Landschaft beschützen; in beiden Fällen ist die Einheit von Haus und Garten gewährleistet. Es gibt dafür zwei Gründe: erstens, der Wunsch, das Erlebnis dieses Hauses als etwas, das größer ist, als man erwarten könnte, erscheinen zu lassen und zweitens, der Wunsch, den Ethos eines besonderen Ortes zu bewahren. Viele der in der Innenraumgestaltung enthaltenen Ideen werden auch im Garten angewendet, wobei man allerdings im Auge behalten muß , daß, obwohl die Struktur des Hauses der des Gartens im Grundriß ähnlich zu sein scheint, die Handhabung des Volumens jedoch anders ist als zum Beispiel in umschlossenen Räumen oder Galeriegeschossen, da sie nur aus Geländeterrassierungen, Anpflanzungen, niederen Mauern, Wasserläufen und sorgfältig angeordneten plastischen Elementen besteht.'

Nach einer Analysis von Deanery Garden schreibt Inskip: 'Es besteht eine hierarchische Anordnung von Räumen innerhalb des umfriedeten Geländes (des Bauplatzes), einer mittelalterlichen Burg ähnlich, die um ihren Bergfried herum angelegt ist. In den meisten frühen Häusern dominiert die Halle, aber nachdem er in Haus Goddards 1899-1910 den außen gelegenen Hof als das Hauptvolumen benutzt hatte, und die Kasematten im Erd-und Obergeschoß, die den Innenraum in Lindisfarne beherrschen, fing Lutyens langsam an, die Gartenterrasse als den Höhepunkt zu benutzen, um den seine Häuser angelegt wurden. Dies steht im Einklang mit der häufigeren Anwendung klassizistischer Stilrichtungen. Diese Entwicklung kann man an vier Häusern verfolgen: Little Thakeham (1902), Heathcote (1906), Great Maytham (1907) und Gledstone Hall (1922). Jedes von ihnen ist symmetrisch um eine Hauptachse in Nord-Südrichtung geplant und mit einer identischen linearen Folge von unabhängigen Räumen die an dieser Achse aufgereiht sind, versehen: Vorhof,-Vestibul, Halle und Garten. Little Thakeham und Heathcote zeigen noch die Tendenz, die Halle zum Höhepunkt nicht nur des Hauses, sondern darüberhinaus der ganzen Anlage zu machen, während Great Maytham und Gledstone den Übergang zum Gebrauch des Gartens als Höhepunkt und dominierendes Element zeigen . . .'

'Während mehrere von Lutyens Häusern darunter leiden, daß sie pompös sind und daß man ihr Raumprogramm sowie das Entwurfskonzept von vornherein kennt, hat er genau diesen Mangel bei seinen besten Häusern vermieden durch den Gebrauch des Paradoxons, und man erfreut sich an diesen Häusern weitgehend, wegen des zugrundeliegenden Widerspruchs einer im Entwurfskonzept etablierten Einzelidee. Die Innenausstattung fördert dies, indem sie gegen die Großartigkeit der architektonischen Baumassen die Einfachheit der Möblierung und Farbgebung setzt, obwohl wenig davon die Chinzwelle in den noch vorhandenen Werken überlebt hat. Baumaterialien wurden meistens gewählt, um die Häuser älter erscheinen zu lassen, als sie tatsächlich waren. Für Lutyens ist Patina ein wichtiger Faktor in der Herstellung ästhetischer Werte.'

Homewood ist das letzte Haus, das Inskip untersucht; er bemerkt dazu, daß es das Paradoxe ist, was Homewood charakterisiert, so wie die Geometrie Heathcote charakterisiert. Obwohl Andeutungen gemacht werden durch das Verhältnis zwischen dem Pförtnerhaus und der Vorfahrt, wird der axiale Zugang zu dem Haus selbst erst auf halbem Wege erkennbar, als die Zufahrt zu einer Andienungsstraße reliegiert wird. Eine große gut beleuchtete Treppe entdeckt man mitten in einer ziemlich niedrigen dunklen Villa, eine klassische Villa als Überraschung innerhalb eines Cottage, das sich wiederum inmitten von formal angelegten Terrassen befindet.

Schließlich muß gesagt werden, daß in vieler Hinsicht Lutyens Häuser als klaustrophobisch erscheinen können. Sie sind so abhängig von der Vorstellung einer Scheinwelt, daß sie die Spontanität der direkten Lösung vermissen lassen, die Lutyens im Werk von Philip Webb so bewunderte, von dem so vieles besonders im Fall von Homewood sich herleite. Während es für das Heim einer verwitweten Gräfin angehen mag, mit romatischem Zerfall zu tun zu haben, scheint die beabsichtigte Vergrößerung das Haus aufzublasen, sodaß der Maßstab völlig überzogen wird und die hermetisch abgeschlossene Welt idiosynkratischer Witze wird womöglich preziös und sogar überbeansprucht in ihrer Monotonie. Obwohl Lutyens Häuser nicht an den radikalen Durchbruch seiner amerikanischen und europäischen Gegenspieler auf dem Gebiet des Entwurfs konzepts heranreichen, ist ihnen oft eine gewisse Brilliance in der Lösung des architektonischen Problems eigen und sie überragen mit Abstand das Werk seiner englischen Zeitgenossen.

Sommario in italiano

Sir Edwin Landseer Lutyens nacque nel 1869. Egli è dunque esattamente contemporaneo di Frank Lloyd Wright, di un anno più giovane di Mackintosh e di 12 anni più giovane di Voysey. Egli ebbe un'educazione normale, tranne per un periodo passato con Gertrude Jekyll allo studio del vernacolo della regione, il Surrey, dopo di che entrò nello studio di Sir Ernest George. Dopo soli due anni cominciò a esercitare a suo conto e tra il 1889 e il 1912 costruì un gran numero di case di lusso. Nel 1912 accettò la committenza per il Palazzo del Viceré a New Delhi, per la quale egli studiò un piano della città insieme a vari altri edifici. Nello stesso tempo cominciò a laborare a dei grandi edifici commerciali nella City di Londra. Dopo la guerra 14-18 egli fu uno degli Architetti Incaricati della Commissione Imperiale ai Monumenti di guerra, per la quale progettò il Cenotafio, il Memoriale ai Dispersi a Thiepval in Francia e vari Monumenti ai Caduti. Tra le due guerre il suo studio si ingrandì e durante la Seconda Guerra Mondiale, eletto presidente della Royal Academy, egli disegnò i piani della ricostruzione di Londra dopo i bombardamenti. Morì nel gennaio 1944, circondato dai progetti per la Cattedrale Cattolica Romana di Liverpool, un edificio che voleva competere con San Pietro per importanza, la cui costruzione fu infine abbandonata nel 1959 a causa del suo costo, quando soltanto la cripta era costruita.

L'articolo analitico di Peter Inskip è centrato sulle case. Egli comincia con l'annotare le varie fonti d'ispirazione di Lutyens; i contemporanei come Norman Shaw, Philip Webb, e ancora Vanbrugh, Hawksmoor, Wren e Palladio. I committenti di Lutyens erano, come quelli di Shaw, uomini avventurosi 'fatti da sè', i quali in generale rispettavano l'architetto per il suo successo personale. Inoltre nel caso di Lutyens la rivista *Country Life*, fondata nel 1897, pubblicava regolarmente il suo lavoro apportandogli clienti entusiasti.

Il programma delle sue case sviluppava l'idea della casa di campagna come ritrovo di fine-settimana con ospiti per brevi periodi. *'In generale le case di Lutyens hanno uno stesso piano di base con (questi) requisiti . . . rispettare l'intimità e il confort degli ospiti con una disposizione gerarchica che divide la casa in zone per gli ospiti, la famiglia e il personale.'*

'In quasi tutte le case è evidente il tentativo di Lutyens di aumentare la grandezza apparente dell'edificio; questo non soltanto nei dettagli dei progetti ma anche nel modo in cui Lutyens organizza i movimenti degli ospiti nella casa. La dimensione è accentuata dal gioco di volumi all'esterno e soprattutto dal rapporto della casa col giardino, spesso inteso come un'estensione integrata alla casa stessa piuttosto che dipendente . . .'

'Volgendoci ora al rapporto casa-giardino . . . possiamo vedere che quest'ultimo ha chiaramente una fondamentale importanza nell'architettura di Lutyens. La struttura geometrica della casa si estende a volte a tutto il terreno, oppure gli elementi del giardino sono trattati come "fittizie" fortificazioni che proteggono le terrazze dalla campagna circostante, e in entrambi i casi il risultato è l'unità della casa e del giardino. Due ragioni appaiono evidenti: la volontà di espandere l'esperienza della casa a una dimensione più grande, inattesa, e il desiderio di conservare il carattere di un luogo particolare. Molti dei principi generatori dell'interno si ritrovano nel giardino, ma bisogna naturalmente osservare che mentre la struttura dei giardini appare simile a quella della casa in pianta, con l'implicazione di volumi chiusi o coperti, il controllo volumetrico è diverso in quanto suggerito dai diversi livelli delle terrazze, dalle piante, dai muretti, dai corsi d'acqua e dalle sculture sapientemente disposte . . .'*

Dopo un'analisi di Deanery Garden, Inskip scrive: *'L'organizzazione gerarchica degli spazi nella parte protetta del terreno è molto simile a quella di un castello medioevale attorno al suo torrione. Nelle case del primo periodo il volume dell'entrata era predominante ma, dopo aver usato il cortile esterno come volume principale a Goddards (1899-1910) e i muri di sostegno, superiori e inferiori, che dominano lo spazio interno a Lindisfarne, Lutyens gradualmente sviluppa l'utilizzazione delle terrazze nei giardini come centro attorno al quale la casa si organizza. Questo trova conferma soprattutto in un uso più frequente degli stili classici. Possiamo seguire questa evoluzione in quattro case: Little Thakeham (1902), Heathcote (1906), Great Maytham (1907) e Gledstone Hall (1922). Tutte sono progettate simmetricamente attorno a un asse principale nord-sud con una stessa sequenza lineare di spazi indipendenti disposti sull'asse: cortile, vestibolo, entrata e giardino. Little Thakeham e Heathcote mostrano un tentativo di fare dell'entrata, più che della casa, il centro di tutto l'insieme, mentre Great Maytham e Gledstone mostrano un'evoluzione nell'uso del giardino come elemento predominante . . .'*

'Mentre alcune delle case di Lutyens risultano pompose e banali a causa del loro programma e dell'uso di uno stesso schema di progettazione, le migliori case si distinguono per l'uso dell'assurdo, e l'interesse di queste case dipende largamente dalla contraddizione di un'idea prestabilita nel progetto.' Gli interni accentuano il contrasto tra la dimensione del volume architettonico e la semplicità dell'arredamento e dei colori, benchè poco di tutto ciò sia ancora visibile, nelle case ancora esistenti, sotto gli strati di tessuto sovrapposti nel tempo. I materiali di costruzione sono scelti soprattutto per dare alla casa un'apparenza antica. Per Lutyens *'la patina del tempo è un fattore importante nella valutazione estetica'*.

Concludendo con un'analisi di Homewood,

Inskip osserva che il paradosso sostiene e unifica Homewood, così come la geometria unifica Heathcote. Benchè suggerito dalla portineria col sentiero d'accesso, l'approccio assiale alla casa inizia solo a metà del viale principale che è improvvisamente relegato a una funzione di percorso di servizio. Una grande e luminosa scalinata appare al centro di una villa piuttosto oscura, una villa classica sorprendente in un cottage, e un cottage vernacolare all'interno di rigide terrazze.

'Infine bisogna dire che in un certo senso l'esperienza delle case di Lutyens può quasi dirsi claustrofobica. Esse sono talmente basate sulle fantasie di un mondo di apparenze che mancano di spontaneità e di quella risoluzione che Lutyens ammirava tanto nell'opera di Philip Webb e da cui soprattutto Homewood fu molto ispirata. Mentre potrebbe convenire alla residenza di una contessa di esprimere una romantica decadenza, questa intenzionale grandezza sembra gonfiare la casa a una dimensione esagerata, e questo mondo ermetico di assurde sorprese diventa forse prezioso e addirittura sovrabbondante nella sua monotonia. Senza realizzare la radicale rottura concettuale dei suoi contemporanei Americani ed Europei, le case di Lutyens spesso arrivano a brillanti soluzioni architettoniche e comunque superano largamente l'opera dei suoi contemporane Inglesi.'

Resumen en español

Sir Edwin Landseer Lutyens nació en 1869. Fué contemporáneo de Frank Lloyd Wright, un año más joven que Charles Rennie Mackintosh y doce más joven que Voysey. No tuvo una educación formal en arquitectura salvo una temporada con Gertrude Jekyll estudiando la arquitectura vernacular que rodeaba su domicilio en Surrey. Ingresó en la oficina de Sir Ernest George y dos años más tarde empezó su propia práctica. Entre 1889-1912 construyó muchas casas notables. En 1912 aceptó el encargo para la casa del Virrey en Nueva Delhí para la cual también produció un plano municipal y varios edificios. Simultáneamente comenzó la construcción de edificios comerciales en el City of London. Después de la guerra de 1914-18 fué nombrado Arquitecto Principal de la Comisión Imperial de Sepúlcros de Guerra, diseñándoles el Cenotafio, monumento conmemorativo a los desaparecidos en Thiepval, Francia, y muchos otros monumentos de guerra. Entre las dos guerras mundiales la oficina extendió la linea de trabajo y durante la segunda guerra mundial, siendo presidente de la Real Academia de Arte, produció planes para la reconstrucción de Londres después del bombardeo. Murió en enero 1944 en la Catedral Católica Romana en Liverpool rodeado de todos sus dibujos. La catedral proyectaba competir en escala con San Pedro, pero la construcción se abandonó a causa de insuficiente caudal, completándose sólo la cripta.

El escrito analitico de Peter Inskip se concentra mayormente sobre las viviendas. Comienza con las principales fuentes de inspiración que Lutyens usó; contemporáneos como Norman Shaw, Philip Webb, y esencialmente Vanbrugh, Hawksmoor, Wren y Palladio. Los clientes de Lutyens, según Shaw, eran 'hombres aventureros, que, en general, respetan a su arquitecto por su propio éxito' pero en el caso de Lutyens fué la revista Country Life, fundada en 1897, que regularmente publicaba sus proyectos y de ésta manera atrayendo a los clientes.

El programa de las casas se desarrolló en torno a la idea de una fiesta de fín de semana en el campo, con visita quedándose para una temporada. 'En general todas las casas de Lutyens tienen la misma planta para cumplir con éstos requisitos . . . respetando el bienestar y la intimidad de la visita con una división jerárjica entre la familia, la visita y los empleados.'

'En casi cada casa, hay indicios de agrandar en apariencia, el tamaño del edificio. No sólo ocurre en la detallada planificación, sino que también en la manera en que Lutyens organizó el movimiento de los visitantes a través de toda la casa. El tamaño se aumentó visualmente en la manera en que están reunidas las masas exteriores y sobre todo en la manera en que se relaciona la casa al jardín, que muchas veces lo considera como una extensión integral de la casa en vez de ser una extensión auxiliar . . .'

'Enfocando sobre la relación entre casa y jardín . . . podemos notar que ésto es claramente de importancia suprema en la arquitectura de Lutyens. La geometría estructural de la casa se extiende por todo el lugar o los elementos de jardín están tratados como fortificaciones "ficticias" protegiendo las terrazas del campo abierto. En éstos dos casos la unidad entre la casa y el jardín se establece. Hay dos razones por esto: primeramente, el deseo de engrandecer la experiencia de la casa a un nivel más alto puede considerarse como apropiado, y segundamente, el deseo de conservar el carácter de un sitio especial. Muchas de las ideas que controlan al arreglo interior pueden aplicarse al jardín, pero debemos notar que la estructuración aparienta la de la casa solamente en el plan, implicando que los volúmenes exteriores son diferentes a las interiores en que sólo estan indicados por terrazas, el arreglo de las plantas, tapias bajas, vias de agua y elementos esculturales cuidadosamente situados . . .'

Despues de lanálisis del jardín del Decanato, Inskip escribe: 'hay un arreglo jerárjico de los espacios en la zona protegida (del lugar) muy similar a la de un castillo medieval. En la mayoría de las casas que primero construyó Lutyens, la sala de entrada domina, pero después de utilizar el atrio exterior como volúmen principal, como en Goddards (1899-1910), y las hileras superiores e inferiores que dominan el espacio interior de Lindisfarne, gradualmente Lutyens elegió la terraza del jardín como culminación alrededor de la cual la casa se dispuso. Ésto es mucho más notable cuando maneja los estilos clásicos. Éste desarrollo puede observarse a través de cuatro casas: Little Thakeham (1902), Heathcote (1906), Great Maytham (1907) y Gledstone Hall (1922). Cada una está situada simétricamente a lo largo del eje principal de norte a sur con una secuencia linear idéntica de espacios independientes arreglados a lo largo del eje: el atrio delantero, el vestíbulo de entrada, el salón y el jardín. En Little Thakeham y en Heathcote podemos ver que Lutyens quiere convertir el salón en climax de todo el sitio en vez de sólo el climax de la casa, mientras que en Great Maytham y Gledstone usa el jardín como elemento dominante . . .'

'Mientras que muchas de las casas de Lutyens son aparatosas y de esperar a causa de su programa y uso básico del plan, sus mejores casas no utilizan ésto por medio de una paradoja, y el placer de éstas depende de la contradicción de la idea en el diseño.' Los interiores acentúan ésto contrastando la grandiosidad del volúmen arquitectónico con la simplicidad del mobiliario y color, aunque poco de ésto permanece. Los materiales de construcción se eligieron para dar una apariencia más fechada de lo que era actualmente. Para Lutyens 'el resultado visible que el tiempo ejerce es un elemento importante para el aprecio estético'.

Concluyendo con una descripción de Homewood Inskip observa que 'es paradoja lo fundamental y lo que unifica a Homewood, del mismo modo que es geometría lo que unifica a Heathcote. El acceso axial hacia la casa, indirectamente aludida en la relación entre el pabellón y la calzada, solo se revela a medio camino y de repente se convierte en acceso secundario. Se descubren unas escaleras bien iluminadas en el centro de una villa obscura y de poca altura, una villa clásica en una casa de campo y una casa de campo con terrazas formales.'

'Finalmente se debe mencionar que visto de varios modos, las experiencias de las casas de Lutyens pueden ser claustrofóbicas. Dependen de una fantasía creada que carece la espontaneidad de solución directa que Lutyens admiró en la obra de Philip Webb y del cual derivó mucho en Homewood. Aún siendo apropiado que una viuda piense en ruinas románticas, el intento de engrandecer, hincha la casa a un nivel engreído. En un mundo de chistes idiosincrásicos se vuelve un poco precioso y su monotonía esta trabajada excesivamente. Sin llevar a cabo soluciones radicales como las de sus contrapartes en Europa y América, no obstante las casas de Lutyens adquieren esplendor en sus soluciones arquitectónicas y encabezan muchas de las obras de sus contemporáneos ingleses.'

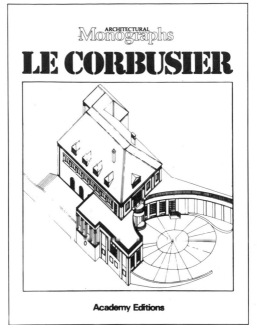

A.D. Architectural Design

ARCHITECTURAL DESIGN is internationally recognised as being foremost among a small number of publications providing up-to-date information on architecture of the present and past. Each issue presents an in-depth analysis of a theme of relevance to architectural practice today, whether it be the work of an important new architect, a currently influential figure or movement, or the emergence of a new style or consensus of opinion. The high standard of writing, editorial selection and presentation has made *Architectural Design* one of the world's most progressive architectural magazines and essential reading for anyone interested in the art of architecture.

Themes covered recently by *Architectural Design* include the polemical work and projects of **Leon Krier**, the theoretical writings and teaching of the Russian Constructivist

Iakov Chernikhov, the **UIA Exhibition** in Cairo, cross-currents of **American Architecture** and the collection of architectural works in the recently opened **German Architecture Museum**. Forthcoming issues include the **Vienna: Dream and Reality** Exhibition coordinated by Hans Hollein, **Tradition: Convention and Invention** by Lucien Steil, and **Designing A House** by Charles Jencks and Terry Farrell.

ART & DESIGN is already acknowledged as the best and only new monthly magazine covering the whole spectrum of the arts. Each issue contains editorial features on the latest developments in art, architecture, design, fashion, music and photography, together with a roundup of news covering products, books, salerooms, gossip, record reviews and extensive list-

ings of both public and private galleries. In addition to the high quality of editorial features by well-known contributors who are experts in their field, the current issues each contain a free original lithograph by a notable contemporary artist. *Art & Design* is available nationally from newsstands each month, or to make sure you get your copy you can take out a joint subscription to *Art & Design* and *Architectural Design* by completing the subscription form below.

A subscription will give you annually six double issues of *Architectural Design* and ten issues of *Art & Design* at a saving of over £20 or $40 on their value if purchased individually. To take advantage of this value-for-money offer, and to ensure that you get your copy regularly, fill in the form below and return it today:

✂ ---

Architectural Design + Art & Design

Please send me one year's subscription to both magazines

UK **£45.00**   Europe **£55.00**   Overseas **US$79.50**. Special discount for students **£5.50/US$10**

☐ **Payment enclosed by cheque/postal order/draft**

☐ **Please charge my credit card account no:** (all major cards accepted)

☐☐☐☐☐☐☐☐☐☐☐☐☐☐☐☐☐ Expiry date . . . .

Signature . . . .
Name . . . .
Address . . . .
. . . .
. . . .

SUBSCRIBE NOW!

Complete the subscription form opposite and return it with your remittance to:

Subscriptions Department
AD EDITIONS LTD
7/8 Holland Street
LONDON W8

All major credit cards accepted